Designing Interactive Strategy

from value chain to value constellation

Richard Normann
Rafael Ramírez

 WILEY

DESIGNING
INTERACTIVE
STRATEGY

About the Authors

Richard Normann is the founder of SMG, a European consultancy advising top management of service and knowledge intensive companies. Of Scandinavian origin, he has lived in France since 1977. Dr Normann holds Master's and Doctoral degrees in Business Administration from Lund University in Sweden, where he was previously a professor. He has consulted to American and Asian firms but is particularly well known as an innovative thinker, challenging conventional wisdom in Europe—from Italy to Finland. Richard Normann is a member of Global Business Network (GBN) and is also a guest professor at Copenhagen Business School. Previous books include *Management for Growth* (1975), *Service Management* (John Wiley, first edition 1984, second edition 1991) and *Knowledge and Value* (1994).

Rafael Ramírez is Associate Professor of Management at Groupe HEC, France's leading business school. He holds a PhD from the Wharton School and a Master in Environmental Studies degree from York University, Toronto. Previously he was 'Chercheur associé' at the Centre de Sociologie des Organisations, CNRS, in Paris (1985–1987). Since 1985 Dr Ramírez has collaborated with SMG, a part of the Swedish Sifo Group, in various capacities, including that of senior partner. He is also an elected member of the Global Business Network. As a consultant, Dr Ramírez has carried out interventions in 20 countries for clients of 15 nationalities. Current research focuses on value co-production, and on addressing complexity.

DESIGNING INTERACTIVE STRATEGY

From Value Chain to Value Constellation

Richard Normann and Rafael Ramírez

JOHN WILEY & SONS
Chichester • New York • Weinheim • Brisbane • Singapore • Toronto

Other Wiley Editorial Offices

John Wiley & Sons, Inc., 605 Third Avenue,
New York, NY 10158-0012, USA

WILEY-VCH Verlag GmbH, Pappelallee 3,
D-69469 Weinheim, Germany

Jacaranda Wiley Ltd, 33 Park Road, Milton,
Queensland 4064, Australia

John Wiley & Sons (Canada) Ltd, 22 Worcester Road,
Rexdale, Ontario M9W 1L1, Canada

John Wiley & Sons (Asia) Pte Ltd, 2 Clementi Loop #02-01,
Jin Xing Distripark, Singapore 129809

British Library Cataloguing in Publication Data

A catalogue record for this book is available from the British Library

ISBN 0-471-98607-0

Typeset in 11/13pt Palatino from authors' disks by Production Technology
Department, John Wiley & Sons Ltd, Chichester
Printed and bound in Great Britain by Biddles Ltd, Guildford and King's Lynn.
This book is printed on acid-free paper responsibly manufactured from sustainable
forestry, in which at least two trees are planted for each one used for paper production

Contents

Foreword

Richard Normann and Rafael Ramírez are practicing management consultants who have written a challenging and useful book about business strategy. They ask the reader to move beyond the conventional wisdom of value chain analysis, popularized by Michael Porter, and based, in Normann and Ramírez's view, on the confining metaphor of the assembly line, in order to enter a less familiar world, created in part by the technology of the microprocessor, of value constellations–multi-partied, interactively dense, dynamic.

In the world of Normann and Ramírez's value constellations, the following propositions hold true:

- The distinction between product and service is irrevocably blurred, since all products carry a periphery of services on which their value depends, and the "hard" product core is better seen as an embodiment of services contributed by the actors that have had a hand in its development. We should think, therefore, in terms not of product or service but of "offerings" that represent blends of both.
- Business offerings are designed in terms of a few key properties. They may be "bundled", so that their elements are inseparable, or "unbundled", so that customers may choose among their elements. A critically important element of an offering is the "code", or pedagogical element, that instructs the customer how to use that offering. Offerings may have the primary function of "relieving" the customer of the burden of performing certain tasks, but winning offerings are designed, increasingly, as "enablers" that enhance the user's capabilities for task performance.
- Relationships between provider and customer are increasingly to be conceived as ones in which the provider helps the customer

create value–at the extreme, taking responsibility for the customer's bottom line. Customers, in turn, are to be conceived not
as passive consumers of offerings but as active contributors to
value creation: without *their* contribution, the value of the
offering could not exist.

• Provider-customer relationships should be conceived not as
one-way transactions but reciprocal constellations in which the
parties "help each other and help each other to help each other."

The propositions and their corollaries reframe our conception
of a business and, with that, the larger economic processes, the
configurations of roles and relationships, in which business is
embedded. Normann and Ramírez argue that their reframing of
the business enterprise carries crucial implications for *design*: for
the design of offerings, which are most effective when they fit the
customer's "business logic"; for the design of business strategy,
which calls for a business logic adapted to, or creating, value
constellations; for the design of the organizational structures
through which strategies are constructed and implemented; and
for the tools and competencies essential to the performance of
these activities–especially the "metacompetencies" through
which managers can integrate, and reconfigure, specialized competencies into coherent business practices.

This book belongs to a genre that might be called "heralding"
or "prophetic"—books that herald the arrival, or prophesy the
coming, of a new pattern in life of a society. Given the power of
what Marshall McLuhan called "the rear view mirror"–our invet-
erate tendency to see the present through the lens of the past–it is
often difficult or impossible to distinguish heralding from proph-
esying: the existing novelty that we have so far failed to notice can
pack a prophetic wallop.

The genre of prophesy may be divided into sub-genres along
the lines of the sociologist, Joseph Gusfield's, distinction between
"Olympian" and "Utopian" social science. Olympian prophesies
like Herman Kahn and Anthony Wiener's *The Year 2000*, and
Daniel Bell's *The Coming of Post-Industrial Society*, are generally the
work of social scientists who maintain a distant, far-seeing, frequently encyclopedic view of the changing patterns they discern
(in Bell's case, the rise of a society dominated by service-oriented,
knowledge-intensive, professionally-based enterprises). Utopian

books (and their dystopian counterparts) herald the coming of a better (or worse) society, and, like McLuhan's *Understanding Media*, and Alvin Toffler's *Future Shock*, they are sometimes delphic—envisaging and proclaiming, rather than arguing for, the occurrence of a radical social transformation. Books like Jacques Ellul's *The Technological Society*, Peter Drucker's *The Age of Discontinuity*, and my own *Beyond the Stable State*, lie somewhere between these poles. Then there are books, written by organizational consultants, whose appeal is wholly pragmatic: they claim to present a new way of understanding emerging patterns of business, management, organization, or strategy and, at the same time, they draw practical conclusions for managers who hope to be effective and to win in the world so described. Into this category fall the work of Edward Deming, to which we owe the now ubiquitous concept of total quality management, Peter Senge's *The Fifth Discipline*, which has helped to popularize the idea of "the learning organization," and Michael Porter's *Competitive Advantage*, to which we owe much of the popularity of the "value chain" and "value added analysis." *From Value Chain to Value Constellation* belongs mainly to this category. And as its name suggests, it is written in criticism of and opposition to the value chain idea. It might very well have been sub-titled, "Against Porter."

The vast popularity of books that herald or prophesy social innovation is itself a remarkable social phenomenon, one that seems to me to be linked to an acceleration of the rate at which ideas in good currency—ideas powerful for action as well as thought—arise, gain ascendancy, and fade away, to be replaced by their successors. When such ideas catch on, they help to shape the worlds they purport to describe. For when people come to see, and believe in, the heralded patterns, they tend to adopt the new language and act on the phenomena so described; and when this process unfolds in the increasingly tightly interconnected organizational ecology of global business, the competitive business game changes in the direction of the patterns heralded by the prophets of transformation. Not surprisingly, the prophets tend to engender countermovements of resistance and skepticism, as illustrated, for example, by Henry Mintzberg's recent book, *The Rise and Fall of Strategic Planning*. Why, the skeptics ask, should we see as radically new a social pattern that has long existed, or give credence to a touted transformation for which the empirical evidence is dubious or non-existent?

Although the delphic prophets often write in a way that seems to defy critical analysis—claiming truth for an idea, as has been said of McLuhan, simply because that idea happened to pass through their minds—certain questions may be legitimately raised about the claims made by any book of social prophesy. First, is it true enough: do the patterns it claims to see present themselves for observation when the reader looks in the right direction? Second, is it useful: when you see the patterns in question, are you able—at least in principle—to take effective action (or to take action that will *become* effective as believers in the heralded pattern begin to make it true as they act in the light of it)? Third, is the message coherent, persuasive, aesthetically appealing: does it tell a powerful story, one that seems to compel the reader's assent?

From Value Chains to Value Constellations goes far toward meeting these criteria. The cases described by the authors—in the fields of health care, home furnishings, and public services, among others—are well grounded in the kinds of evidence that practicing consultants are usually best able to adduce. And these cases are supported, in my own observations of organizations in fields such as pharmaceutical and information processing, by examples of firms that have succeeded, or are busily engaged, in redesigning their offerings and relationships to customers so as to take far greater than usual responsibility for their customers' creation of value. The book is useful. Managers would do well to examine their offerings, business strategies and organizational designs in the light of it. The book's usefulness is enhanced by the fact that it is timely: its key ideas are clearly beginning to be held and enacted by managers and consultants, yet these ideas have by no means peaked. And the authors have succeeded in weaving together an appealing and compelling story of business transformation—one to which many readers will probably pay the ultimate compliment, namely, that of regarding its message (in retrospect) as obvious!

What Normann and Ramírez have not done is to provide the reader with a critical and productively skeptical treatment of their own findings. They do not present us with challenging, alternative explanations of the business patterns they herald, nor do they attempt to assess the limits of their applicability. But this omission is pardonable: prophets are not generally held accountable for failing to consider the arguments against their prophesies! In any case, as the authors' ideas are taken with increasing seriousness— as I suspect they will be—economists and business scholars will probably come forward to do the job for them. In the meantime, managers, consultants, and interested observers of the rapidly evolving world of business will find this book provocative and instructive—an important addition to the sparsely inhabited category of management books that contain usable knowledge.

Donald A. Schön
Cambridge, Mass.
March 1994

Foreword to paperback edition

This book is important and worthwhile reading for many reasons. The authors are addressing and developing some fundamental and powerful ideas and concepts.

I have had the opportunity to lead business organizations in three different cultural contexts—Sweden, France and U.S.A., and within two corporate cultures—Volvo and IKEA. I have learned that successful and outstanding organizations are, with few exceptions, driven by a challenging mission, a meaningful purpose and shared values.

This meaningful purpose for a commercial organization must be to create and deliver:

- Customer value
- Coworker value
- Social value
- Shareholder value

A company delivers true customer value when it enables customers to do something with their lives that is better, easier, or more valuable than any other company can offer.

A company or an organization delivers coworker value when it enables its coworkers to grow as individuals; making the time spent working rewarding beyond the paycheck.

A company delivers social value when people beyond its customers, coworkers, suppliers, and shareholders recognize that the company is instrumental to build a better world to live in.

It is my firm belief that when a company creates and delivers the values above, financial growth and growth in shareholder value will follow because people will give and give freely. This will fuel the energy needed to create outstanding financial results.

The value creation process of any company is therefore linked to its capacity to enable its customers, to enable its coworkers and suppliers; to enable the greater community to accomplish something valuable.

This is what I find to be the main idea of this book; that customer value creation has to be seen as when companies with its products and services are enabling their customers to create value. By substituting coworkers for customers we add another dimension, with the same principle.

This book, *Designing Interactive Strategy—From Value Chain to Value Constellation* provides a framework for shifting focus from the actual activities performed by a company—the value chain perspective—to the activities to be performed in order to enable customers to create value. One of the Normann and Ramírez's key statements is that value is not in the objects or in the actors buying, but in the actions of both, that is in the interaction. This gives a very different and powerful perspective compared to what is normally practiced. It is an outside-looking-in perspective giving new insights to the definition of what business a company really is in, to what key capabilities that are needed, and to understanding how to get organized in order to deliver.

Exemplifying from my own experience, this 'enabling perspective' helps clarify whether Volvo is in the business of selling cars and trucks or in the business of creating car and truck ownership satisfaction. With the first definition the relation with our customers ends when the car is sold. With the second definition the relationship starts. There are obviously very important differences in what we as an organization should focus on, what we should measure, what magazines we should read, etc. . . . given the first or the second perspective. To further clarify the important difference I have frequently used a quote from a Revlon President of the 1950s, 'Yes indeed, in our factories we are producing lipsticks, but in our stores we are selling hope.' It helps to see the difference from focusing on the product to focusing on the purpose of the product. In the IKEA world this means shifting from 'selling furniture' to 'helping people make a home out of their apartment/house.' Again this makes a dramatic and decisive difference in how IKEA sets out to design products and services and how IKEA presents itself in catalogues, stores and advertising.

IKEA is used in this book as one of four case studies to support the author's hypotheses. The unquestionable success of IKEA can be explained in many different ways. However, the capability to deliver high quality at a low cost is in my view the most critical explanation. This is made possible by three unique IKEA processes:

- IKEA—the global networking organization
- IKEA—the prosumer organization
- IKEA—the empowered organization

In all three processes, value is created and co-invented—the global networking case with a close relationship to the suppliers, the prosumer relationship with customers and the empowerment through inviting coworkers to a constant ongoing experimenting innovation process built on openness and trust.

To give further support to the authors' theories and to their conclusion on the uniqueness of the IKEA concept I can share the STOR case. Briefly, STOR, Inc. was a copy of the IKEA concept presented as three stores in Los Angeles, California in the late 1980s. American professional retailers identified IKEA as having 'broken the code' and they wanted to roll out the concept in the U.S.A. before IKEA. The copy was very complete and well done from products, product names, store layouts, children's playroom, catalogues to Scandinavian flags. A very ambitious and impressive work. However, the problem was that they copied only the surface. They never understood the underlying power of the three co-producing processes mentioned above. To mention only a few examples, they never established the same supplier partnership built on an in-house design capability, they rather excused themselves for the Ready to Assemble (RTA) approach than making that a key feature of the value equation, they prepared their stores for self-serve and not for self-choice (i.e. where you enable customers to find, choose, and buy products on their own) and they never understood the importance of the catalogue as an instrument for customers to plan at home before coming to the store. The STOR story started with some commercial success, but ended with financial failure.

This book is interesting and enlightening also because it helps to build a bridge to other important theories, like systems theory, and the theory of learning organizations.

One of my key mentors and source of inspiration is Professor Russell Ackoff. He has taught me for over 20 years the enormous price we pay when we break apart problems to make complex subjects more manageable. We can no longer see the consequences of our actions since we lose our sense of connection to a larger whole. He is a master on explaining why the defining characteristics of a system cannot be understood as a function of its isolated components, because:

- the behaviour of the system doesn't depend on what each part is doing but on how each part is interacting with the rest;
- To understand a system we need to understand how it fits into the larger system which it is a part of.
- How we define the parts is fundamentally a matter of perspective and purpose, not intrinsic in the nature of the 'real thing' we are looking at.

Rather that thinking of a world of 'parts' that form 'wholes' we ought to recognize that we live in a world of wholes within wholes. Rather than try to 'put the pieces together' to make the whole, we ought to recognize that the world is already whole.

Systems thinking helps us understand that we indeed create and shape our own reality and our future in the interaction with our environment and not by a consequence of events created by somebody 'out there'.

Another source of inspiration of mine, Peter Senge, teaches us to see a company as a living system, capable of recreating itself. This is to understand one of the key prerequisites for building learning organizations where one constantly learns how to learn and how to develop things together; sharing knowledge and information. Learning is a process of recreating ourselves as individuals and as organizations. Through learning we re-perceive the world and our relationship to it. Through learning we extend our capacity to create, to be part of the generative process of life.

Learning is rewarding and very powerful, because accumulated learning is exponential. The more an organization knows, the faster it learns. The faster it learns, the more it knows. This is very much in line with the Value Constellation perspective presented here by Normann and Ramírez. They argue that companies build their re-configuration skills on two assets: (1) Customer bases (relation to customers supporting customer value creation) and (2) Competence enhancement. The reconfiguring meta-competence is to ensure that assets (1) and (2) develop each other as much as possible in a continuous interactive learning process, an effective dialogue between competence development and customer development.

Finally another reason why the ideas of this book are so powerful is the growing relevance of its ideas for the emerging new world of tomorrow. The digital revolution we are witnessing is driven by technical breakthroughs in the information technology giving us rapidly increasing capacity for information transaction, at rapidly decreasing costs. This development has given IT a new critical meaning since they wrote the book (1994) *From Information Technology to Interaction Technologies*.

The Internet will not only change the content and the amount of information available, but most importantly, it will provide a new metaphor for decentralization, a new way of thinking about many other things in our lives.

We are about to move from an old to a new logic, we are shifting focus from things to ideas, from seeing organizations as machines to seeing organizations more as communities, from hierarchy to networks, from a Newtonian to a quantum logic, from information technology to interaction technology, from action to interaction. Customers will be more active. Business will be more interactive. This change is dramatic with profound consequences for all of us, as nations, regions, companies, families and individuals.

It seems to me that the framework for value creation that Normann and Ramírez have presented is capturing a very fundamental aspect of this change. The shift from a linear value added perspective to a multidimensional co-productive value constellation perspective.

As the authors say, 'Customers in the emerging economy attain a strategic significance far beyond that which traditional microeconomic theory attributes to them. Taken within our co-productive framework, they are active partners in the joint value-creation process, not simply passive recipients of the value creation of others'. (p.78)

It is easy to agree and to understand why this book is worthwhile reading.

Goran Carstedt, PhD
Former Head of IKEA Europe, President of IKEA North America Inc., President of Volvo Svenska Bil AB, President of Volvo France S.A. Cars

Preface

Business is being re-invented. We understand *business* to be *activities* which create value and *management* to be the *organizing* of those activities. Economics teaches us that value creation implies the judicious utilization of resources which are—virtually by definition—scarce.

Technology is changing the relative scarcity of resources, as it has done many times in the past. These changes in relative scarcity, which represent a discontinuity in relation to the past, change priorities: old high-priority, and thus relatively scarce, resources become less critical as new, higher relative scarcities emerge and gain higher priority.

It is the technological discontinuity-driven business re-invention that is driving the many changes in management we are now witnessing: process re-engineering; total quality management; just-in-time; 'lean' production; de-layering; risk management, including the use of ever more sophisticated derivatives; the 'learning organization', and so on.

This book's purpose is to examine the nature, or 'logic', of business as it is emerging from this discontinuity. While the consequences of the changing logic of business for management activity *are* outlined, they are not the focus of the book. This has a price to it: the book may appear to be 'unpractical'. But it is our view that getting a good hold on the 'why' and 'what' of business is very useful for doing the 'what', 'how', 'with whom', and 'when and where' of management. For this it is convenient to review our understanding of strategy.

Strategy prepares organizations to best create value under future conditions, which may not be entirely known in advance. Strategy allows business people to identify opportunities to bring value to customers, and to devise ways of exploiting these opportunities. Strategy does this through the provision of frameworks, models and ideas that ground these opportunities, rendering them understandable and communicable. In this respect, strategic processes explicitly define what 'business', what value creation, a company is in.

But just as business is being re-invented, so is strategy: the rules of strategy making are also undergoing a fundamental change today. Much recent strategic thinking has been based on the assumptions and models of the industrial economy. Value production activities in such models have been located along a 'value chain', which is a model representing an assembly line. Individuals, departments and whole companies have had their relative positions located along 'value chains', those *'upstream'* from the unit in question have been termed 'suppliers', those *'downstream'*, 'customers'.

Like a portrait which, over time, dictates to those who see it how the person portrayed actually looked, models also tend to transform what they model, constraining that reality within the limits of the model's logic. With value chain models it has become almost impossible to consider a supplier as a customer, or a customer as a supplier, for the value chain model has inherent linear, unidirectional and sequential characteristics which it imposed on the reality it modelled. In the value chain model, value is not really *'created'* any more, it is instead *'added'*, step by step. Here, to produce value one receives something from one's 'supplier', 'adds' value to it, and then passes it on 'downstream', to one's 'customer', be it an 'internal' or an external one. Much of value production, when seen in this way, in fact is nothing other than cost adding; and the very sense of 'value' has tended to be limited to the 'cost adding' which the model allows for. Many functional units such as training or advertising in firms whose business has been modelled in value chain terms thus know how much they cost, but not how much value they create.

Microprocessing and related technologies, and the social transformations they have catalysed, an example of which is the break-up of AT&T, have created new options to produce value which cannot be 'mapped' with the linear (one-dimensional), unidirectional and sequential limitations characterizing the value chain. Words like 'synchronous', 'parallel', 'concurrent', 'distributed', 'co-processed' or 'co-produced' denote the new possibilities which break the time, space, interface and role constraints inherent in traditional strategic models. The discontinuity is at least as fundamental as the advent of Henry Ford's assembly-line production revolution. It is the modelling of such possibilities to create value with which this book is concerned—and it concludes by outlining the managerial consequences it holds. In the end, it is the very nature of the firm as we know it which must be reviewed.

In changing the 'value chain' concepts of strategic thinking, one changes not only the model but also the very conception of what strategy, of what business, of what value creation and its organization, and indeed of what economic value itself is.

We argue that in the emerging business environment, winning companies become business redefiners, often even redefiners of the 'industries' they are in. These companies do not decide what businesses they will be in—they invent and re-invent the business from scratch, and are ahead of others in redefining the roles and relationships which will make that new business definition work. They use a different language from conventional companies, they use different units of analysis to survey the business they are in. This is true for the company as a whole and is also the case for sub-parts of companies, such as divisions, strategic business units and even departments.

The full implications as to the 'how' of this game are being designed and redesigned today and provide a fascinating possibility for research and innovation. It is in the hope of catalysing such changes that we are writing this book today.

Paris, France,
December 1993

Acknowledgements

The origin of this book is a multi-client study that the authors conducted for some twenty European international companies in the late 1980s. The point of departure was that the very nature of business is changing, and so the study came to be called 'Business Logics for Innovators'.

We owe a great deal to those clients with whom we learnt as we reported our findings. Very special thanks go to Kees van der Heijden, then at Group Planning in Shell, and now a professor at Strathclyde University, for his constructive criticism, encouragement and uncanny ability to identify and amplify many of our most important hunches.

The team conducting the original study within our group—SMG—was much larger than ourselves and made important contributions over a long period. We are particularly indebted to Frank af Petersens, Anders Holst, Sigurd Lilienfeldt, Kaj Storbacka and Caroline Drevon.

Many professional colleagues outside our group provided invaluable advice and forced us to clarify our intellectual position. In particular, thanks go to Tom Teal, Robert Howard, Bill Taylor, Allan Webber, Vincent Carroll, Donald Schön, Eric Trist, Jaap Leemhuis, Charles Hampden Turner, Erik Johnsen, Larry Hirschhorn, Paolo Celentani and Tom Gilmore. Michael Brady, Rachel Amato, Chris Murray, Diane Taylor, and Kristina Boman helped at various stages to elaborate and finish the manuscript. Thanks too, to the *Harvard Business Review* for allowing us to use the title of our 1993 article for this book.

We want to thank all the above, and the many others whom we cannot list here, for their help and contributions. Special thanks to Fabienne Autier for the preparation of the second edition.

PART ONE

The Historical and Technological Driving Forces Shaping Business Today

1 Introduction

Business is changing its logic. This must be understood before changing management practice, processes or structures.

We believe that making the difference between the world of management and that of business is useful. In an ideal world, the two, of course, match each other. Tasks needing to be done in the world of business, by which we mean a domain of value creation, require the co-ordination that management provides.

Ideally, the way the managerial world evolves would match the changing realities of the world of business tasks. Business evolves over time, for the demands it must meet in changing socio-technical and competitive contexts themselves evolve. The transformations in the fundamental logic of the world of business which this evolution brings about calls for matching transformations in the fundamental logic of the world of management. But this does not happen in the way one would like it to, for the world of management is institutionalized.

As MIT professor Donald Schön stated in his 1971 book *Beyond the Stable State*, the institutions that make up the world of management tend towards what he called 'dynamic conservatism'. The bureaucracy which characterizes much of the world of management creates 'friction' for the evolution of the fundamental logic, preventing it from evolving. Instead of continually matching the evolving logic of the world of business, the institutionalized and bureaucratic world of management becomes ossified, and is often a key 'brake' for business evolution. Manager's minds become more preoccupied with the managerial situation, and thus the mind-set also prevents organizations from adapting to the changing business environment.

As business evolution occurs at different rates over time, with, for instance, technical breakthroughs producing sudden and discontinuous changes; there are some stages of corporate evolution where the difference between the world of business and that of management becomes particularly noticeable. In such situations, the misfit between the logics of the ossified managerial structures and the dynamic business realities that they are supposed to co-ordinate create gaps. In the end a new managerial co-ordination support system must be put into place. But before that, fundamental rethinking of the business logic is required. This is the subject matter of this book.

Any company with a 10-year-old department in charge of managing what microprocessing does knows this type of problem. From the electronic data processing (EDP) departments of the batch-processing days, the world of management of this part of the firm has gone through various changes which are known today by names which typically include the words 'Information', 'Systems' and 'Networks'. The gap between the world of management and that of business that we are experiencing today is of the same kind but of a different order of magnitude. It is a gap which concerns not only the single department or division, not only the single firm or corporation, not only the single industry or sector, but also the whole economy. It is a change of phase that is as comprehensive and far-reaching as the change which the Industrial Revolution brought about. Yet, as opposed to the many decades over which the Industrial Revolution took place, this change of business logic is making itself evident in a much shorter period of time. This means that the need to comprehend its logic and to develop a world of management that better fits it is a matter of urgency.

It is because of this urgency that we launched the study 'Business Logics for Innovators' in 1986, the result of which is this book. It has taken us this long—8 years!—to understand the nature of the new logic well enough to convey it in book form. Our research leads us to conclude that the fundamental logics, the conceptual frameworks, governing much of the existing world of management is fundamentally out of phase with the emerging logics of the world of business. The conceptual framework of the world of management prevalent in most companies, in its many variations, is inherited, as we will see, from an era in which the assembly line was the primary referent by which value creation took place. While assembly lines still exist, technological innovation and other factors reviewed in this book are transforming business activity and its possibilities. Assembly lines are no longer the primary mode by which value creation takes place, even if in many companies they are still important components of production. As activities based on other social and technical configurations become ever more important in diverse value-creation processes, the alternative logics which they have at their core make the assembly line-based referents ever more exceptional. Basing one's overall view of the value creation on the assembly line, which is now but a small part of the overall value-creation system in which it is embedded, is thus misguiding: a more relevant framework, better fitting the overall value-creation process, is called for. This is what this book offers.

2 Competitive dominance in the world of business

At its origin, economic activity was based on extracting raw materials, whether natural or mineral, and trading them. Key success factors in this 'extract and trade' economy related to securing access to the raw materials: the right location, the necessary extraction tools, and means of transportation to make them accessible to others.

In the early stages of this economy, these success factors were more usefully thought of in comparative rather than in competitive terms. An economic actor based in Jamaica would deal in sugar cane and rum since those were the raw materials available at that site. In Newfoundland, the industry would be centred around fishing. The two industries did not compete, but they each had a comparative advantage (access to raw materials) over each other in their respective locations, leading to win–win trade.

The pre-industrial, artisan-based, and then the industrial economies which followed were centred on a different activity from the original 'extract and trade' economy: the transformation of materials and resources into products. The passage from the one to the other naturally changed the key success factors. Raw material access control, centred on geographic location, so important in the agricultural–mineral economy, became less crucial. In the transformative economies, one could convert wool into sweaters in many locations, independently of where the sheep were located. As Larry Hirschhorn has argued so well in his book *Beyond Mechanization* (1984), technical progress has been a process whereby economic actors have been progressively released from constraint, step by step. Thus, in the emerging transformative economy, a key success factor for a while was securing access to river and wind energy sources (e.g. in milling), but with the invention of the steam engine, this energy source factor for location became relatively less important. Gradually, securing geographical and energy access gave way to securing access to knowledge as a key success factor (cf. Normann and Ramírez, 1989; Wickström and Normann, 1993). Access to the pasture for the sheep, then access to the source of energy, gave way to the importance of 'knowing' how to better transform the wool. The acquisition of *production* knowledge became an important basis for success in the early phases of industrialization.

In the industrial economy, the way resource transformation occurred in production included Adam Smith's (1776) '*task specialization*'; in fact, much of such transformation was centred on this notion. With industrialization, the craftsman who produced the complete product from start to finish was gradually replaced by workers specialized in certain tasks. Adam Smith used the example of a pin, which in the pre-industrial economy would have been made completely by one pin-maker. In typical industrial production, one worker makes the head, one the tail, and a third glues the two parts together. These three specialists make many more pins than three craftsmen making entire pins over the same period of time. An accompanying feature of this industrial process is that each part of the pins thus made must be the same, so that any of the heads can be glued—assembled—to any of the tails. This *standardization*, made famous by Henry Ford's assembly-line production of identical (black) Model T Fords, thus came to be a second key characteristic of industrial production, together with task specialization. With this standardized production, unit costs came down, enlarging the possible market for products, which in turn allowed large investments to be made in production: *mass markets* and *mass production* thus became characteristics three and four of industrialization.

Economic success is based not only on producing but also on selling what one has produced. The most talented knitter in the world will not have an economically successful business if she only knows how to knit wonderful sweaters. She must know how to get customers to buy them too! While Henry Ford recognized the potential of the car buyers' market, and through the mass production of the assembly line was able to meet that potential, he became trapped in his thinking by this system. This trap is best summarized in a statement that is attributed to him: '*The customer can have a car of any colour so long as it's black,'*—(see Halberstam, 1986 for an account of Fordism). Beyond production knowledge, a key success factor in industrialization became the efficient use of resources to ensure sales of what is produced. *Marketing* knowledge then became a more crucial success factor than production knowledge, a phenomenon we have seen develop until very recently. Increasing one's market thus became the next natural step in critical success factor definition, particularly in terms of successfully attracting a competitor's customers. General Motors with its cars of different colours and shapes and sizes began stealing actual and potential Ford customers—which enhanced the creating of new car purchasers that Ford's mass production insights had catalysed.

This book is about the next stage of critical factors, the stage beyond industrial era marketing. We will see that key success can be made to depend no longer on production or marketing knowledge advantages but on the use of other assets that in the industrial form of economy, of value creation, remained unexplored and underutilized. To 'discover' the new-found importance of these assets, we must re-evaluate the picture of the world of business as described by the current models of economic activity, which we have inherited from the industrial era.

3 Economies versus sectors

In the early 1930s the world of business was neatly divided by researchers trying to make sense of industrialization into three types of activities, which came to be known as *'sectors'*, as Gershuny and Miles (1983) of the Science Policy Research Unit of Sussex University have observed. The *primary* sector was defined as agriculture and mining, the original raw material extraction and access-based type of industries that have existed since the beginnings of economic activity. The *secondary* sector was defined as industrial manufacturing, which covered the transformation-based production industries with specialization, standardization and mass production/mass markets described above. A diverse group of activities not fitting the characteristics of these first two sections, including activities such as transportation, distribution, restoration and healing, were 'lumped' into a *third* category or 'sector', which was called 'services', and which in effect had no cohesive logic except that its activities did not fall into the other two sectors.

This 'sector' notion has survived until today, and is widely understood to encompass economic activities characterized according to their *output* (Normann, 1984, 1991). The weakness of this categorization is that it has become increasingly evident that the outputs of the secondary and tertiary sectors, goods and services, respectively, can no longer be neatly separated. The original differentiation between goods and services was simply that the former was a 'tangible' output (like a car), while the latter was an 'intangible' output (e.g. health).

In their study on the transformation of employment in industrial societies Gershuny and Miles (1983) note that the traditional three-sector model used to map economic activity 'describes a world much simpler than the one we actually live in', adding:

IF agriculture delivered food directly to the households which actually consume it and employed only farm labourers...
IF manufacturing industries employed only manual workers...
IF the service sector employed only white-collar workers producing final services directly for their ultimate recipients...
THEN the three-sector model would give us a powerful description of the process of development of economic structures.

Therefore, they suggest, 'for more complex modern economies we need a rather more sophisticated theory'.

As Gershuny and Miles argued in terms of employment, and as we propose here in terms of value creation, with the economy that is now emerging, this goods/services distinction no longer holds, causing the 'sectorial' model on which it is based to be inaccurate, unhelpful and misleading.

While industrialization was epitomized in the assembly-line manufacturing of tangible goods such as Henry Ford's Model T, it has gradually been recognized that industrial production necessarily included services, such as accounting, purchasing, insurance for workers, materials and equipment, and delivery of finished products. All these 'production costs' are 'service activities'; as emerging economic patterns make their 'outsourcing' common, the *'tertiary'* nature of these *'secondary'* production costs is rendered more visible. The core 'secondary' sector thus becomes tied to the 'tertiary' one. Thus, instead of thinking that goods-based wealth from the secondary manufacturing sector allows society to enjoy tertiary 'services', it is now becoming evident that efficient 'tertiary' activities make or break the 'secondary' sector. Researchers on the other side of the Atlantic have also shown that the greatest growth in tertiary activities, services, takes place within the secondary economic sector, manufacturing. Thus, James Brian Quinn and Christopher E. Gagnon of Dartmouth stated in a *Harvard Business Review* article (1986) that

More money is often made in the goods sector through information and services than through production activities...In fact, one study shows that about three quarters of the total value added in the goods sector is created by service activities within the sector.

This underlying weakness of the division of goods and services has become ever more evident in recent years to virtually everyone.

It is almost self-evident that many products today are packages of what was once sold as services. For example, one can buy a compact disc of Luciano Pavarotti in any music store, rather than paying for a concert ticket to hear him at Carnegie Hall. Desktop publishing hardware and software purchased from Apple replaced the services bought from printers.

In a previous book, Normann (1984, 1991) added a second dimension to the original *sectorial* dimension in the three-sector model: the dimension of economies. In the model as drawn in Figure 3.1, activities in the service 'economy' take place as much within the 'primary' agriculture and extraction, and in the 'secondary' industrial manufacturing sectors as within the 'tertiary' service sector itself—an observation consistent with the research cited above.

	Agricultural sector	Manufacturing sector	Service sector
Agricultural economy			
Manufacturing economy			
Service economy			

Figure 3.1   The three-sector model

If 'sectors' refer to fields of activity defined by its *output*, 'economies', on the other hand, are based on *type of activity or process*—specifically, the mode of operating and the way of organizing and structuring value-creation activity. The car industry can be placed easily (and misleadingly) in the industrial manufacturing sector since its output is a tangible good. When we begin to look at 'processes' with the intention of placing the industry in one or another of the three economies, we realize how misguided the sector categorizations can be. For it is immediately evident that most of the process of manufacturing and selling a car today takes place within the service economy for most manufacturers. About a quarter of the retail price of a typical car is related to direct manufacturing costs, and this excludes the costs incurred by the buyer after she starts using it!

Seen in this way, services do not comprise a set of value-creation activities different from manufacturing. Services will never re-place goods, hence our opposition to labelling the current economic age 'the service economy' in a 'post-industrial' sense, which would imply that all activity is going to be service-centred. However, as the manufacture of goods becomes more service-intensive, the concept of sectors becomes outdated, and thus irrelevant and misguiding. This is certainly the case in business, and may quickly also be the case for statisticians cataloguing national economies.

With the 'economies' view of value-creation activity, the agricultural economy is seen to depend on rent economics. The industrial manufacturing economy is based on scale economics, characterized by mass production and markets, standardization and specialization. It is captured conceptually in the 'value chain' concept, which depicts the assembly line, this economy's most typical form. Here value-creation activity is sequential and linear, with actors 'adding' value to what they receive 'upstream' and passing it 'downstream' to the next actor.

In this book, we describe the emerging service economy: here the provider helps the customers to create value, and does not simply sell them products or services made previously.

Before we begin our core discussion of 'value-creation logics' with which we depict the emerging economy, we describe the key technological developments which, like the steam engine with industrialization before it, triggered the transition to the emerging service economy. In the following chapter, we describe briefly how the microprocessor is the key technological driving force shaping this emerging form of business.

4 The microprocessor

We have above referred to Hirschhorn's (1984) view on how technological evolution implies constraint removal. The invention of the steam engine freed production sites from the constraint of the location of natural energy sources, such as water, which forced mills to be built next to rivers or streams. In the same way, steam power required bulky levers, belts and pulleys tied to a single main drive shaft connecting steam engine to production technology. These production 'machines were highly constrained, single-purpose in character and design and hard to modify' (Hirschhorn, 1984). They were limited to the fulfilment of one function, at a given speed, and were placed in the factory in terms of how they could best be connected to the drive shaft.

The invention of the electric motor broke these steam engine constraints: 'To change the relative speeds of different production equipment sections, the mechanic or engineer, instead of stripping the machine and replacing old gears and cams with new ones, need only adjust the relative speeds of the different electric motors, (Hirschhorn, 1984). The electric motor thus allowed the factory layout to reflect the rational flow of materials through the factory, placing machines in a way that more closely fitted production/transformation process requirements, rather than energy distribution constraints.

The removal of constraints through technological innovations creates choice. In the industrial era this choice creation was obtained by *separating* functions, what Hirschhorn called *'functional dis-aggregation'*. The invention of the electric motor allowed the *transmission* of energy to be separated from *movement, speed* or *direction*. Machines were no longer limited by a single energy source, but with their separate energy sources became 'independent' of each other, thus free from the constraints of breakdown or adjustment in any one level, thereby improving the productivity of capital in a remarkable way.

As opposed to the electromechanical developments of the early phases of industrialization, microprocessing technology development is based on a different logic: it provides extra choices through the reintegration of functions in one machine—*functional re-aggregation* has replaced functional separation (Hirschhorn, 1984). Disaggregation meant that one had the choice of using machine A to accomplish task A or using machine B to accomplish task B, or using both machines at the same time to accomplish both tasks simultaneously. Re-aggregation means that it becomes possible to group tasks A and B (and any multitude of other tasks) in one machine. This multiplication of tasks into one unit is accomplished through the programmable microprocessor. Microprocessing technology can perform not one or two tasks but millions in fractions of a second which, together with optical communication and storage makes activities and resources widely available for others.

The groundwork for microprocessing was laid with two twentieth-century *knowledge* developments, respectively *integrated feedback theory*, which led to the body of knowledge we term 'cybernetics', and the invention of *the vacuum tube*, which is a gate-like mechanism that operates, as Hirschhorn puts it, as a sort of 'electric venetian blind' that conducts a larger or smaller electric current. Such developments permitted the signals from gauges and other sensors such as X-ray machines, to be integrated as coherent instructions that are fed back to devices, such as valves and pumps, which regulate the production processes. These breakthroughs enabled amplification, modulation and frequency response to act in concert. The first electronic computing machine was built in the 1930s at Iowa State University (cf. Pava, 1982, 1983). The vacuum tube was still the basic computer building block in the early 1940s, when 18 000 of these were used to build ENIAC (electronic numerical integrator and computer) at the University of Pennsylvania. In the late 1950s, vacuum tubes gave way to semiconductor transistors and these in turn to integrated circuits; multi-transistor junctions integrated on the same piece of silicon (the first 'microchips'). In 1969, Intel designed a programmable central processor that was embedded in a single chip of silicon and which replaced eleven separate integrated circuits. The 'microprocessor' was born.

Like the invention of the electric engine, the arrival of the microprocessor implied that a very large amount of flexibility had been accrued per unit of investment. Clearly, this invention implied incredible reduction of costs…but the impact of the chip would be far greater.

Microprocessing technology Part One: the density of options

Microprocessing technology, as opposed to mechanical and electromechanical technology, allows machines to perform multiple functions. The built-in redundancy is thus a redundancy of functions, not of parts,[1] as a given part can be programmed to do several tasks. A common example of microprocessing technology is a personal computer, with which one can type *and* edit words, perform arithmetic *and* make drawings; and it is even 'smart' enough to give warnings such as 'diskette is full, please save on another diskette'. But this technology is now embedded everywhere—from 'smart' coffee makers to credit cards.

Microprocessing technology is not simply one more 'step' in the evolution of technology, as it entails a fundamental new direction of its development. For almost two millennia, technical advances were limited to mechanical improvements, no matter how spectacular. Microprocessing technology breaks from mechanical improvement to offer a range of options unimaginable before the microprocessor. For example, an author is writing a book during an afternoon. His ability to create value depends on his intellect, in part, of course, but also on the resources available to him at that time. A crucial resource for a writer is something to allow him to transfer his thoughts into words that can be read by others: editors at first and eventually readers. A hundred years ago, the writer would have probably used pen and paper. Fifty years ago, the pen and paper would have been replaced by a typewriter, a mechanical invention. Today, a writer will

---

[1] This distinction was originally made by Fred Emery.

most probably use a personal computer based on microprocessing technology.

The improvement of the typewriter over the pen and paper was limited. The typewriter mechanized the pen, and in so doing, it standardized the type, improving readability, and increased writing speed, enhancing labour productivity. Paper was still necessary, paragraphs could not be 'moved' once they were placed on the paper, mistakes had to be erased, and the manuscript was still sent in paper form to the editor. While the typewriter had not added any new functions to the process, it eliminated some functional constraints and added others, as, after all, a pen is much more portable than a typewriter.

With microprocessing technology, the writing process has not only been rendered more efficient, as with mechanization, it has also been significantly changed. A personal computer not only allows a misspelled word to be corrected, but has also added the option of finding the misspelled words, moving words and paragraphs at will, changing the typeface and layout after the writing, creating diagrams and allowing us to place them and replace them where wanted, etc. In principle, with a modem and the right printing equipment, one can send the document electronically to a print-shop and have a print made within minutes of having finished the manuscript. While modern offices and newspapers work in this way, the institutionalized bureaucracy of organizations to which we refer above are slowing the pace with which such possibilities become widely available in the book business.

Personal computers are not all alike. Some are bulky deskbound affairs, while others are the size of a 'notebook' which can fit into any briefcase. If an executive is at his or her desk, we can safely assume that the PC's options will make her choose a PC over a typewriter to accomplish her task. If she is in a plane, then a portable PC would be much more valuable to her than a deskbound PC. The number of options for action and interaction available within a time/space unit is what we call *density*. At a desk, a personal computer has greater density than a pen; in a plane, a portable PC has more density than a non-portable.

Any actor in a business situation—anyone creating economic value—functions in the dimensions of time and space; his or her position can be defined in terms of time/space co-ordinates. His ability to create value depends on how the characteristics of the time/space territory he travels and inhabits correspond to possibilities for actions and interactions with other economic actors. If resources in his time/space unit are few, constraining and/or poor, then his activity possibilities will be correspondingly limited.

We saw how the executive's action possibilities were enhanced by a 'dense' portable computer. Let us expand that example. It takes less than an hour by plane from Paris to London. With transportation to and from airports, and the necessary procedures at the airport, this time probably at least quadruples. It takes our executive four hours, plus or minus, to get from city centre to city centre.

The time/space the executive is dealing with is four hours, in an aircraft, airports and taxis. Eighty years ago an offering to position the activity of moving from the city of Paris to the city of London in the time frame of four hours would probably have been thought of as a miracle, but today's business executive may well think of it as a nuisance; a waste of time, of money, and of opportunities. Therefore there is stiff competition and many attempts to improve the offering.

One such opportunity is, of course, to decrease the travel time, which might be possible by direct city centre to city centre airborne transportation, or by taking a near-supersonic high-speed train through the Channel Tunnel and above ground. Another is to replace human physical movement with moving human images with video-conferencing techniques. Not surprisingly, the microprocessor is helping people to advance along all three of these routes.

More conventional ways of dealing with the time dimension implies giving the business executive special treatment at check-in desks and lounges while inefficiency on the part of the provider system's way of handling this dimension 'steals' time from her. Much effort goes into 'enriching' the time she is made to spend, attempting to make the availability of breaking away from physical constraint somehow compensate for undue temporal constraint. Thus telephones and faxes are installed in planes, lounges and taxis; business publications are made available to enable her to do things that she would have presumably done elsewhere, hopefully freeing other units of time/space for other activities.

It should be noted here that increasing *options* for an activity in a given space/time situation is not identical to increasing *actual* activity. A higher density of options may also mean the option of not doing a given activity. In the illustration above, our business executive may choose the option of not being disturbed, throughout the flight, in order to sleep. The built- in multi-functionality of resources allowed for by the microprocessor makes the option-enhancing density increase possible. It is this that converts the airport lounge into a waiting place, *and* a communications centre, *and* a writing and learning centre, *and...* creating new activity options.

Programmable microprocessors have changed the way we travel, learn, communicate, and even eat. Pre-cooked frozen dinners placed in pre-programmable ovens or popped into microwave ovens avoid the need to shop for and prepare the neccessary ingredients. But they also make it possible for you to serve Michelin three-starred chef Michel Guérard's cooking to your mother-in-law in your very own home, saving you the expense of travelling with her to his restaurant in south-east France. Access to Guérard's talents and experience without leaving home—at *any time, any place, no matter*, as Stan Davis (1987) put it—is what microprocessing-based constraint breakdown brings to you.

Microprocessing technology Part Two: asset liquidity

Activity to create value is the basic building block of business. Business is the practice of economics inasmuch as value creation implies using resources that are scarce in order to create value. Assets are the accumulation of value-creating activity; this accumulation allows further such activity to take place. The more effectively this further activity can happen, the more valuable the asset.

In the agricultural economy, as we saw earlier, some assets such as secured 'ownership' of location access are *combined* with others such as extraction or agricultural equipment to extract raw material assets which are traded. In the industrial manufacturing economy, the combining of assets process is similar. Assets which embody productive knowledge, be they people or production processes, are *combined* with other assets (for instance, physical production facilities) to create assets which are traded.

Electromechanical technical breakthroughs, such as the steam engine or the electric motor, removed, as we have seen, several time and place constraints determining how assets could be combined. The new set of conditions such constraint removal created gave rise to industrial manufacturing. The technical breakthrough which microprocessing obtained revolutionized economic activity because it further freed time and space barriers to asset combination.

As our simple example of the business executive with the PC showed, she could combine available assets such as experience, knowledge and information into a new asset (an investment plan, for instance) almost anywhere. She could do the necessary calculations, however complex, with the support of financial programs in the computer's hard disk, as well as write out the plan for approval by others using word-processing software also in the computer's hard disk. With a sufficiently advanced computer she could digitally fax this information to the relevant people, regardless of where they were and what time it was in their locations, ready for them to decide upon it almost as fast as she finished transmitting it. If the computer has a cellular modem in it, she can do this while she is still in the plane—and change it according to the opinions of others on the ground, who can fax her their opinions!

The microprocessor has not only redefined time and space dimensions in the production process, it has also changed the 'media' used. In the above example, paper is not used except by readers on the ground: the writing instrument is also the calculation and communications (or 'information') instrument. Microprocessing technology has not only affected the way the business executive carries out the actual production of her investment plan, but also the access that she has to several assets. In this example, these include the opinions of experts and colleagues around the world, the calculation tools developed by many professionals in the past which have been converted into software packages, different information sources and databases, editorial assistance in her computer's word-processing software, and so on. Her personal computer can be said to be a *'dense'* offering because it offers all these different options to her in such a small time/space unit, that is, because of its inherent multi-functionality. It can also be said to be *'dense'* because of its capacity to enable the business executive to access all those many different assets which are otherwise so spread out in time and space on a 'here and now' basis. It 'densifies' options into a very compressed time/space dimension, suiting her own value-creation actions. Also, because the asset she is producing (the investment plan) and the assets she uses to create this can go so easily to and from her computer to the computers and minds of many other economic actors, as these assets can *'flow'* virtually anywhere at any time, microprocessing also contributes to making assets *'liquid'*.

'Density' and 'liquidity' are two crucial characteristics of assets which microprocessing has obtained. Neither of these characterisics were as relevant in the past in shaping business development as they are today. The impact of liquidity is not limited simply to enhancing temporal and spatial availability; access is not only faster, but in many cases it allows actual access to happen for the first time. Thus, previously unused or underutilized assets, such as relevant information, become valuable additional assets in the economic activity. Liquidity 'awakens' value in assets which was 'dormant' and underutilized prior to the microprocessor's appearance.

This is illustrated by how the Italian fashion designer and producer Benetton has emerged into a worldwide commercial success. Microprocessing technology allows Benetton to analyse the transactions in key stores around the world. As its business is centred on being at the core of changing fashion trends, it becomes crucial to know which styles and colours are selling the most where. The better Benetton can read and reinforce existing trends, the better it is at its value creation. As a result of the intelligent use of asset density and liquidity, Benetton has been able to develop a very quick response time in product development. As soon as their computers detect a developing trend, they adjust their production to reinforce that trend in that location, helping their customers to be more effective in their own business, which in this case is to become successful trend-setters.

Thus Benetton has converted a simple customer-transaction record, previously used for accounting and fiscal purposes only, into a dense and now extremely valuable asset that can be exploited to help customers to become successful; in so doing, the customers help Benetton itself to become successful. This book is concerned with the creative use of these newly available asset characteristics, 'density' and 'liquidity', in developing winning business ideas and practice.

PART TWO

Value Constellations

Section A Co-production

5 What is a product?

One of the authors was recently listening to music by the French composer Charles-Valentin Alkan, using a new compact disc (CD) player. The CD player, of an American make, comes in three boxes. One box is a digital-to-analogue decoder of a design that is said to deviate from that of competitors' products, based on experience of working with state-of-the-art computers of the person whose trade mark the CD player bears. Two more boxes are the actual mechanical player and its separate power supply. Although all three boxes carry the same trade name, the mechanical player itself has been manufactured to customized specifications by a Japanese company known for its superb knowledge of mechanical engineering. The laser pickup comes from another Japanese company considered a leader in that field. Many of the other components, including the digital signalling chips, are supplied by well-known American companies. Part of the software from the several minicomputers which form part of the system is licensed from a small, Wisconsin-based company. The thick aluminium panels have been chosen on the basis of experience gained in space applications.

The music by a French composer, played by a British pianist, recorded by a British international company, encoded on a disc made according to a patent by Philips and Sony, is innovative while obviously building on the state-of-the-art of musical thinking as defined by Beethoven, Chopin, Schumann, Liszt and other great nineteenth-century composers.

When combining the CD player unit with the other elements of the audio system, and with the CD itself, the listener is provided with access to a great range of knowledge and experience developed by a large number of artists and professionals in many corporations from different countries, by some of the world's greatest composers, and by the scientific and humanistic traditions that they built on, respectively. This experience, this knowledge, has been accumulated over many years and around the world. It is incorporated into the three boxes which, together with other physical manifestations, form a product system. Via this physical medium, the listener has access to all that experience, which has been built up by very knowledgeable people performing a very large number of different types of activities.

However, the listener would not have had access to these accumulated activities if the product had remained in the inventory of the French importer where it was a week before the author played the CD. Closing this 'access gap' took place through the combined activities of a number of hi-fi journals, advertising agencies, the best audio dealer in Paris, at least two banks, an experienced technician, transportation of the units with the technician and an impressive range of electronic measuring equipment via a van of French manufacture, as well as the primary school teacher who taught the author to read and count and several key activities carried out by his parents! Also, the product would not have been there unless the manufacturer and the dealer had not made a commitment to service it in the future to secure long-term functioning and reliable access to all the resources at hand.

Metaphorically we can easily think of this 'three-box' product as the physical embodiment of assets comprised by knowledge and experience, in themselves the result of myriad activities performed by many people dispersed in time and location. Some of these activities have provided access to natural resources in increasingly refined forms. Others have produced complex goods and systems. Others again have created knowledge of basic technologies and sciences. Yet other activities have combined many of these resources in a systematic way, and created access to them for users. Although the aluminium front panels are remaining physical evidence of much of the activities that the user now has access to, the transportation, financial services, advisory, installation, management, and other activities have been equally necessary and indispensable in making the user able to enhance his life by listening to Alkan. It is thus useful to consider any 'good' as the physical embodiment of an incredibly complex set of activities performed by a very large number of actors.

Any 'service' follows the same logic. Without dissecting a service (say, a visit to the family doctor) in as much detail as the CD player, we can summarize some of the activities which make the service possible. By meeting the doctor, the patient has access to the accumulated experiential or clinical knowledge of that doctor and, through the doctor's own history and education, to relevant parts of the accumulated knowledge of medical science. Since the consultation cannot be performed without physical objects—the hospital or room in which it takes place, equipment such as the X-ray machine or stethoscope—in the consultation the patient also has access to all the activities embodied in those goods.

In sum, a product or a service, anything of value to a 'customer', is created through a collection of activities by different actors made available in one way or another to the 'supplier' bringing value to the customer. Since the same logics apply to both product and services, we will henceforward use the term *'offering'* to refer to any *output* of a value-creation system (the 'producer' or 'supplier') that is an *input* to another (the 'customer').

6 Density of offerings and value creation

Offerings, as we showed earlier, have become *'denser'* as they offer more options for the customer's own activity. Technological advances manifested in denser offerings often result in the reduction of the number of activities which the customer of the offering must perform to do something; sending a fax from a personal computer requires one to do fewer tasks, and requires one to mobilize fewer actors, than sending a letter. At the same time, the multiplication of choices inherent in enhanced offering density can mobilize a greater number of actors and actions if all options are activated.

We have shown how an offering (goods and/or service) is the result of a complex set of value creating activities involving different actors working together at different times and locations to produce it for and with a customer. We now look at how the different actors in a value-creation system enabling offerings to be produced relate to each other as offering density increases.

Because of the increasing number and variety of 'options' inherent in and embedded within the offering, the relationships among actors are changing. The 'interfaces' among these that are constantly being redefined as asset liquidity make it possible to reallocate activities from one actor to the next. In fact, it is the very invention of new offerings to which this interface innovation process gives rise. The new offerings in turn push economic actors such as our airborne business executive with a portable PC to reconsider their existing interfaces, their roles and their relationships with other economic actors (Van der Heijden, 1993).

In his influential book *Competitive Advantage*, Michael Porter (1985) depicted the relationships between actors in a productive system in terms that were uni-directional and sequential in nature. In Porter's now-famous 'value chain' notion, economic actor A sells (or passes on) the output of his work to actor B, who 'adds' value to it, and sells or passes it on to actor C, who adds value to it, and sells or passes it on to actor D, and so on until it is sold to the end consumer. But with microprocessor technologies, economic actors are increasingly engaged in sequential *and* simultaneous activity relations with other economic actors. Insurance policy guidelines for a new car warranty might be drawn up in Hartford and its advertising campaign designed in New York while the car is still being manufactured in Detroit. After the new owner has an accident with the new car, the after-sales service of the manufacturer, the claims division of the insurance company, and analyses of which message to give to future buyers are simultaneously being carried out—and all bring value to car users.

Even when our analysis is limited to the manufacturing portion of the creation of a car, activities once performed sequentially are now, through microprocessing technologies, performed simultaneously. The Peugeot 405, for example, came out one year faster than its predecessors: Peugeot developed many versions of the car simultaneously through the use of computer-aided design (CAD) systems integrated with computer aided manufacturing (CAM). Concurrent engineering, distributed processing and many other such microprocessor-based innovations are systematically replacing sequentiality with simultaneity.

Economic actors no longer relate to each other in the simple, unidirectional, sequential arrangement described by the value chain notion. The relationship between any two actors tends to be far more complex than can be conceptually captured by the unidirectional 'make/buy' model underlying the value chain. Instead of 'adding' value one after the other, the partners in the production of an offering create value together through varied types of 'co-productive' relationships.[1]

---

[1] It should be noted here that we are not in any way dismissing the value chain and other sequential models as irrelevant to today's business world, but rather as limited. This can be illustrated by an analogy. The concept of the earth as being flat still works in limited cases, like designing a table or going for a weekend drive or rolling out asphalt on shopping-centre parking lots. But it is hardly a useful concept for running an airline. For practical purposes the flat earth concept may be thought of not so much 'wrong' but rather as of limited applicability, as a special case of the broader topology which the round earth view affords. Likewise, the concepts we discuss in this book go beyond the value chain, which has its roots in a world that is now a special case of a broader value-creation topology. For limited purposes, with enough constraints, and within a limited time frame, the value chain is still useful, just as flatness is a reasonable concept for limited areas on the earth's surface. In addition, the value constellation concepts of this book cannot be reduced to adding up interconnected value chains any more than the round earth concept can be explained by adding up flat earth views. See our comments to this effect Normann and Ramírez (1993b).

In 1967 Thompson described three types of relationships between parts of an organization. The most simple one is what he termed a 'pooled' relationship, in which the different parts each contribute to form a whole. The second type of relationship is what he called 'sequential': sections of the organization produce parts which are then inputted into another part. The dynamics of this type of organizational interrelationship are very similar to the value chain process as described by Porter. Finally, Thompson described the 'reciprocal' relationship, the most complex of the three. In this case, the outputs of each section of the organization become inputs to the sections from which they get their own inputs. Thompson showed that all organizations have pooled relationships between their different parts, as everyone in a given organization is working together towards a same goal. Complex organizations have pooled and sequential relationships, while the most complex organizations, according to Thompson, have all three types of relationships in them.

Applying Thompson's categories to the system of value-creating actors, we can see that the value chain covers the first two types of relationships. It does not, however, provide the conceptual framework to describe the more complex interaction among different actors which liquification and density, through the removal of temporal and spatial constraint, have brought to bear upon their interfaces: the 'reciprocal' relationship.

Co-production is the term we use to describe the 'reciprocal' relationships between actors which characterize the service economy. We describe co-productive relationships with the help of examples below. In the following chapters we explore in detail aspects of co-productive systems which render them effective.

7 Examples of co-production

In the car industry in Europe, national distributors represent the manufacturer's interests in a given country. They are the key interface with the dealers with whom the public deals. It is the point of this book to show that if a customer were to buy a car directly from a car manufacturer, he would be acquiring something different from that which existing distributing arrangements allow him to purchase.

In traditional value chain terms, the car manufacturer is a provider of value to the distributor, who acquires this value, to which it presumably adds further value as measured in value-added taxation. It then passes this added value on to the dealer, who does likewise before selling the offering to the individual in return for money.

However, as we have seen in the Benetton example, the microprocessor has today rendered the relationship possibilities among the four actors much more complex. The business opportunities offered by the co-productive view of their relationship are not even considered by a value chain perspective. A good dealer provides the car distributor and manufacturer not only with money but also with many other strategically crucial forms of value. For example, it can supply information about its local competitors, about what cars customers trade in, about how they use vehicles and how they make buying decisions. These help to design cars, dealer-support packages, insurance schemes, advertising and marketing campaigns and many other activities making for win–win–win relations among them. In other words, the dealer helps the car distributor and manufacturer to design better cars and related systems which should help the dealer to be more profitable.

The four actors create outputs which are inputs to the other three; not just those 'downstream' from oneself. The inputs enable every actor to become more effective. Multi-directional reciprocity structures this example: any two of the actors involved help each other to help each other to help each other...to help others. And the commercial relations among the four actors are not simple make/buy ones. While economic actors in the value chain are linked to the player before and after in the chain, in the co-productive view the links are multiple. The manufacturer is linked not only to the distributor but also to the dealer, for example by providing dealers with comparative data on how well they are doing in their region, as well as internationally, in relation to changing customer trends. This enables the dealer and its customers to have a more effective co-productive relationship. Volvo in Sweden, for instance, helps local dealers to determine elements in their relationship where they are relatively weak *vis-à-vis* internal benchmarking studies. Local dealers present this information to their customers, and 'contract' with them on what specifics they will improve over a given number of months. This creates goodwill and enhances the sense of quality on which they compete.

8 The customer's customer

Let us look at another example of co-production[1]. In North America, McKesson is the largest health care supply management company. The company provides health care products and services to pharmacies, hospitals and health care networks. McKesson is also one of the largest distributors of bottled drinking water. McKesson's way of working together with its customers is the focus of our attention here. Although McKesson was a leader in this industry and it was generally considered to do what it did very well, they found that they had fallen into a trap. Independent pharmacies were being acquired by large chains of drugstores. Given this trend, the wholesaling function was being performed more and more by the vertically integrated chains, leaving less space for companies like McKesson. As a result, in the late 1970s, McKesson came very close to selling its pharmaceuticals wholesale and distribution businesses.

But instead of selling the business, McKesson reacted by switching the view of its business from a traditional 'value chain' logic to a co-productive one. This new view was centred on an in-depth understanding of the business situation of its customers. In essence, McKesson said: *If our customers are not strong enough to survive in the face of new competition, it must be because they and us together do not have the appropriate co-productive relationship.*

McKesson, in effect, decided that it would offer pharmacies something other than what it had provided up to then to enable its clientele to survive. 'Your success is our success' was the slogan it adopted.

McKesson took the perspective of the independent pharmacy, looking at its resources, market and business situation. In so doing

---

[1] This case concerns a time period closed in 1994.

it realized that to provide value to their customers, the independent pharmacies, they had to enable the pharmacies to better 'connect' with the pharmacies' own customers. The sequential order of activities inherent in the value chain view was no longer helpful here. If the independents wanted to remain independent, rather than sell out to chains, McKesson would need to help them to achieve just this. But in doing this, McKesson did not only 'add' new value to its customers. As we will see below, its innovations really changed the nature of its business: it became much more than an efficient 'wholesaler'.

9 What is a business?

McKesson were able to redesign their offering because they had enlarged their view of their relationship with their customers to include the one their customers had with their own customers, the patients. This led them to enlarge the field they considered to many other actors; for instance, by viewing the logic of the patients, they saw that most of what they spent on their own, or 'direct' customers, the pharmacies, came from health insurers. These paid the pharmacies later, often much later, than the moment the patient acquired the drug from the pharmacy. Cashflow was therefore a weak link in the pharmacist's business. McKesson restructured payment relations so that cashflow would no longer be as much of a problem for the independent pharmacist that wanted to engage in this 'survival' adventure. McKesson looked at how the pharmacy related to other actors: it discovered, for instance, that pharmacists had to do considerable paperwork not only for the payer (the insurance company) but also for ordering, stock-keeping, the regulators, and so on. McKesson thought that applying microprocessing 'density' and 'liquidity' advantages to these tasks would make a great difference, not only to the pharmacist (greater efficiency and lower unit costs) but also to the patient, as it freed resources in the pharmacy from administration that could be deployed for greater service and advice availability.

In a systematic way, McKesson went about analysing which parts of the pharmacy's activities before, during and after purchase were what we term *cost carriers* and which were *income or price carriers*. It also analysed which activities in each of these three instances were manifested in people, which in goods, and which in 'systems' enabling customers to engage in 'self-service'. Our interpretation of this approach, which is depicted graphically in Figure 9.1, implies a wholistic picture of a given business, in this case that of McKesson's clients.

Product	Before purchase	During purchase	After purchase
Manifested physically			
Manifested in people			
Manifested in systems			
Manifested in client			

Figure 9.1 A picture of a 'whole' business of one's customers

Instead of manifesting McKesson's relationship with the pharmacies in the 'make/buy', 'output/input' terms inherent to the 'value chain' view, the emerging economy framework we offer here allows it to be seen as a co-productive interface manifested in twelve distinct but interdependent ways. The 12-square diagram depicts an 'offering'; McKesson could replace 'cost-carrying' and 'price- or income-carrying' elements in each box as it saw fit; particularly if it considered the pharmacy's 12 boxes, its own 12 boxes, the 12 boxes of the patient and/or his or her insurer, and various other actors' 12 boxes.

Boxes in Figure 9.1 with 'cost-carrying' activities that have no corresponding 'price/income carrier' are given away 'free', or 'bundled', with the rest of the offering. Offering redesign means replacing the cost and price-/income-carrying composition in the 12 boxes within and among economic actors; this is exactly what McKesson did.

While McKesson continued to believe that the provision of pharmaceutical products to the pharmacies remained its core business, it realized that the new business situation of its customers required this reconfiguration of activities within and among economic actors, and their cost and income 'bundling'. McKesson exploited the economies of scale and scope it enjoyed in relation to its pharmacy customers in, for example, efficient ordering and processing of insurance-based billings. But because it understood that, for its customers, 'independence' was valuable as they would have otherwise sold out to chains, it offered these 'broadened' offering possibilities in an unbundled form. The pharmacy could continue to buy pharmaceuticals without buying the other elements of the offering, and could opt out of any arrangement within 30 days if it so desired. The 'survival-enabling package' which McKesson developed and offered to pharmacies consists of many parts which can be bought as one system or separately. Yet pharmacies signing up for the one-month renewable 'survival' package typically increased the volume of the pharmaceuticals distribution business they had through McKesson by an average of some 30%.

The flagship element of the newly broadened offering was called *'Economost'*. *Economost* allows the individual pharmacy to know how well it is selling each product. It suggests the optimal placement for the different products on pharmacy shelves in self-service pharmacies, and prints out tailor-made pricing labels. This last element is called *'Econoprice'*, and is also available unbundled. The mass-produced individualization aspect allows pharmacists using *Economost* ordering to relate the order to delivery packaging in ways that fit the specific outlay of the ordering store. The unpacking can thus be made along the aisles of the store, reducing delivery-to-stockage delays and saving time.

'Econotone' is a similar competitiveness enhancer for smaller pharmacies. It offers the ordering element but does not include price stickers. *'Econocharge'* provides pharmacists with credit control and accounts-receivable management. *'Econoplan'* helps pharmacists with their marketing activities and *'Econoclaim'* helps them to handle insurance and government claims, improving their cashflow, advancing insurance-financed sales payments one week on average.

Much of the knowledge-based assets which McKesson transferred to the pharmacies it embodied in physical 'technical' forms such as computer terminals. It prevented its clients from switching to substitutes by ensuring that it started down the experience curve before anyone else realized what constituted that curve; at the same time, it induced customers to co-produce some of the value. Thus, customers must, to some extent, tailor-make their business to fit the competitiveness-enhancing offerings that McKesson has designed. This means that self-serving customers invest in staff training time, and develop a new way of operating, fitting McKesson's new offerings. This increases customer loyalty and the 30-day opt-out clause makes this appear risk-free independence enhancement. For McKesson this clause has the advantage of allowing them to know how well they are doing within a very short feedback loop.

All elements are both cost and price carrying, which means that they can be offered unbundled. They are all designed to be profitable on their own, but, as we have seen, together they are even more profitable, as they increase the share of market within the customer that McKesson secures for itself.

McKesson has applied the same strategic understanding that it developed for the interface it had with its 'customers' to its 'suppliers'. Electronic ordering systems give pharmaceuticals firms a better indication of demand, enabling them to better manage inventories. McKesson, for instance, helped Eli Lilly & Co. to reduce turn-around times from 10 to 14 days down to about three.

10 Shifting activities among actors: reconfiguration

As value-creation systems involve more than one actor, they entail a division of labour. Actors help each other, and help each other to help each other, to perform their respective activities. As a value-creation system is freed by technical and social innovation from pre-existing constraints, and from the limits which the sequential chain view of events supposes, possibilities for assigning activities to economic actors in the system become much richer. This makes given or established activity configurations less robust and more volatile.

Not only are the different actors 'helping' each other to accomplish their respective tasks, but in co-productive relationships, the very architecture of tasks can itself also be co-produced, reassigning activities to different actors. With this holistic view, enhancing the effectiveness of a given way of dividing labour is *a significant optimization problem* (Van der Heijden, 1993) which is in fact how business development takes place, as we will see below. Activities once only assigned according to technical/functional or short-term financial priorities (the manufacturer builds, the wholesaler sells) can be reassigned if value is thus somehow improved (i.e. through lower unit costs; enhanced availability or variety; or, as we see in the example below, more effective risk-sharing).

Key to the way activities are reassigned are the concepts of *'relieving'* and *'enabling'*. The 'goods'-based value chain notion implies a relationship between supplier and customer which is, primarily, a 'relieving' one. Here the supplier will do something, such as building a plane, *for* the customer, relieving him of having to build his own plane. Yet more and more businesses are moving from a relieving logic to an enabling one, where the 'supplier' does something that makes it possible for the 'customer'[1] to do what it does better. For instance, the French aerospace and armaments company Dassault- Breguet, faced with a significant decline in the sale of its military aircraft at the end of the 1980s, decided to enable the Indian Aeronautical Development Authority (IADA) to build its own light combat aircraft instead of selling it French-made fighters. The manufacture of the Indian aircraft thus involves an innovative sharing of activities between the French 'supplier' and its Indian 'customer'.

An even more telling example, more fully explored in the third part of this book, is the case of IKEA. Customers select, pick up and assemble the IKEA-designed furniture themselves. Thus customers 'relieve' IKEA of the task of assembling and delivering the furniture, which IKEA 'enables' them to do for themselves by providing customers with excellent catalogues, large parking areas near the store, trolleys to carry the packages to the cars, assembly instructions and tools, pre-drilled parts, etc.

In both these cases, the value resulting from a redefined co-production is optimized. The Indians receive French technical know-how, avoid paying for French manufacturing costs, and create value more effectively, strengthening India's air force at a lower price. The lower unit costs of IKEA's innovative reconfiguration also allows reduced prices for the IKEA customer.

Activities are increasingly reassigned not only to lower unit costs and to fight inefficient cross-subsidies but also to optimize risk-sharing, risk-absorption and risk-management. Van der Heijden (1993) has found a neat example of this regarding how car manufacturers guarantee the bodywork of a car against rusting. From the single-year warranty of yesteryear, now guarantee periods have become much more extended, sometimes for as long as 10 years. With galvanizing and other rust-protection innovations at the pre-assembly stage of manufacturing, 'suppliers and manufacturers,' van der Heijden explains, 'implicitly agree that covering the risk of corrosion is a lot cheaper for the manufacturer, who only needs to make a modest modification to the production

---

[1] 'Supplier' and 'customer' are in quotes, as in co-productive relations the terms are increasingly misguiding: both actors are 'supplier' and 'customer' of each other. Money values the value differential between them when it is perceived to exist. When it does not, one has a 'barter' relationship.

process, than for the car buyer, who has no other option than buying a new car if things go wrong'. The risk of corrosion-handling activity has shifted from the car purchaser, who in Nordic climates used to have to spray the underside of the car with messy chemicals prior to every winter, to the manufacturer, who is much more effective at doing this.

11 Innovative co-productive relationships

Car manufactures co-produce value with insurance and financing companies to provide the customer with a complete, competitive package. Such partnerships are now common for a car company; but note that co-productive partnerships are now extending established industry definitions. Thus, Porsche also co-produces with sunglass manufacturers and watches to sell the Porsche image. Porsche's innovative relationships with other actors goes further. Realizing the potential of its engineering know-how, Porsche began selling its knowledge to non-competing manufacturers, such as Volvo and Seat, who needed to accelerate development programmes. Seat also capitalizes on the Porsche image as anyone who opens the bonnet of a Seat can find out. Porsche understood the power of this and extended it: its engineering can be found in Lindé forklifts and Airbus cockpits. Organizationally much of this sharing of knowledge is administered via the Weissach Engineering centre. While continuing to support the development and manufacturing of Porsche cars, it sells its engineering services to many other economic actors.

Innovating in the effective use of 'density' and 'liquidity' through unprecedented co-productive relationships has increased the importance of so-called 'off-balance sheet' or 'intangible' assets such as brand image and inherent knowledge; partly because these imply a more effective risk-sharing arrangement. Seat is not simply taking Porsche's know-how and adding value to it; Seat and Porsche are working together to create a more effective way of converting their respective cost carriers into competitive income-generating, price-carrying offerings.

Today's world of business is becoming so interrelated that many actors are involved in co-production without consciously realizing that they are working together. This means that many strategic opportunities are seriously undervalued, sometimes dangerously so. When Volvo stated several years ago that it liked Saab to sell so many cars in the United States, as Saab enhances the awareness Americans have of Swedish cars, Volvo was in fact saying that it benefited from something it gets from Saab's relationship with US customers and for which it (Volvo) did not pay. Saab was, in effect, co-producing an image with/for Volvo, for free.

Relationships in co-production are thus more complex, more multi-directional and simultaneous than those in the industrial business world as described by the value chain. Actors are no longer just buying an item, adding value to it, and selling it to the next link of the chain. Instead of adding value one after the other, the partners in the production of an offering create value together through inventing new relationships, as the examples above illustrate. In the next section, we explore in more detail how co-production brings enhanced value to the customer.

PART TWO

Value Constellations

Section B   Offerings and Value-creation Logics

12 Introduction

In his book *A Brief History of Time* (1991) the celebrated British physicist Stephen Hawking reviews some of the most fundamental questions of our existence. How did the universe come about? How does it function? How is it evolving? These are questions, pertaining to Einstein's Theory of Relativity, which concern some of the most powerful processes imaginable. Paradoxically, the key to understanding these *macro* processes according to Hawking appears to lie in the discoveries of quantum mechanics, an area of physics concerned with the *smallest* contexts we can conceive. In other words, the keys to the very large 'reconfigurations' of the universe are to be found in the ways micro-reconfiguration, resulting from the forces governing the relationships between the smallest particles, operates.

In our search for a new framework for business strategy we have found it useful to take an analogous approach. To understand the ('macro') emerging economy, we must take a critical look at the very nature of economic transactions, the 'micro' level of analysis. In the course of this inquiry we will find that the way whole industries are being reconfigured can be usefully linked to changes in value creating among economic actors at the 'micro' (or 'elementary particle') level of human action and interaction.

The 'macro' level in this analysis concerns the way value-creating activities are organized between *institutions*, which develop relationships with one another and which can be identified and categorized according to the patterns they form. Thus some patterns have traditionally been known as 'industries' or 'sectors of economic activity'. We have indicated earlier that such 'sector' definitions are losing their significance in a world that is rapidly being reorganized, and that few organizations can be readily classified according to the old categories. Furthermore, the advent of a multitude of new co-productive relationships in the form of alliances, joint ventures, outsourced subcontracting, franchising, etc. has reshaped not only individual organizations but also the patterns that organizations form in relation to each other, rendering existing definitions of an 'industry' or 'business' equally outdated and misleading.

If a broader level of institutional change reflects how transactions between actors in the marketplace are changing, this is centred on the fact that institutions live by exchanging value, and this exchange is in the end still based on the principle of comparative advantage. Transactions concern 'offering' exchanges between two or more actors. As offerings change, as they become more co-productive, so do institutions that transact them. Take the following two postulates: an organization can create only offerings which reflect its capabilities; only organizations whose capabilities reflect the basic value creation logics of the marketplace can be competitive, and thus survive. Hence, long-term survivors are institutions whose evolving business logics reflect the market's (changing) value-creation logics, and which manage to create viable offerings in consequence.

To understand these 'macro' phenomena in greater depth, however, we must look to the equivalent of the atoms, subatomic particles and related 'micro' interactive forces in the economic universe. We must investigate these smaller particles and their interactions, and attempt to establish what causes them to change and manifest themselves in new ways. It is by studying the basic laws governing these microprocesses that we can discover the emerging nature of value creation and how the configuration of effective new value-creation systems are constituted. Changes at this micro level are manifested in the marketplace as offerings and consequently, on the macro level, in reconfigured institutional structures and arrangements.

13 The micro level—a first look at its architecture

Let us begin with some basic economic principles. The ultimate goal, if not the very nature, of economic activity is to create value. Value is produced by humans acting with each other and using the resources that are at hand; previous activities are made available for further action to this effect.

Economic transactions concern the exchange of activities and/or resources which carry a price tag. These prices denote the differential between the activities by the supplier and those the customer must perform to gain access to, or ownership of, the supplier's activities. Users are prepared to pay for the resources/activities that are made available to them because they somehow enhance the effectiveness of their own value creation, for instance by lowering costs or by making it possible for users to do things they could not do otherwise. We have suggested earlier that value can be measured by the 'density' of options, as manifested in the knowledge, resources and activities made available to the user in time and space. Note that, for our purposes, the three concepts of 'knowledge', 'resources' and 'activities' are equivalent, although they are manifested in a variety of ways in time and space for each user. As we will see below, the choice of how these three are rendered accessible to each user is a key element in business development.

As we saw earlier, the production, or rather co-production, of value in the emerging service economy is manifested in offerings, to which several actors contribute by performing specific activities. The offering is the physical and 'in-person(s)' embodiment of assets made up of knowledge and experience, in themselves the result of myriad activities performed by many people dispersed in time and space. Assets and resources imply the *storage* of activities which have been configured for a particular purpose, for a particular actor in a given location at a given time. Some of these activities have secured access to natural resources in increasingly refined forms; others have created complex transformations of such resources, making products and subsystems possible; yet others have developed knowledge of basic technologies and sciences; all these having been combined in a systematic way, in the end ensuring access to them for users. Thus, in the final analysis, whether customers buy a 'product' or a 'service', they really buy *access to resources*.

The distinction made in the industrial economy between 'products' and 'services' obeyed the following logic: activities packaged into physical goods were more readily amenable to the scale economics of the mass production of that era. They were, in effect, an efficient way of storing activities by sharing the cost their creation represented among many price-carrying manifestations which could be matched by as many revenue-generating customers. Service activities were less easy to design so as to benefit from such economics; scale was only achieved when they were 'productified', as in the case of trust or unit funds which were found to efficiently 'productify' costly financial advice in many distinct (if identical) units which were price carrying, and which could be individually sold to many individual revenue-generating customers.

Inasmuch as customers pay for their share of the value-creating activities that have taken place 'behind the scenes' of what they buy, the cost of all such 'behind the scenes' or 'back-shop' activities is 'bundled' into the price of the offering in ways reflecting the offering's value-creating architecture. While the cost in all cases reflects the activity configuration in the offering, in the industrial economy the price was most closely attached to the *physical* embodiment of the supplier's activity, that is, the 'good'. Where services were concerned, the price was typically more linked to *activities*, be they those performed by the 'supplier' (e.g. a clown in a circus) and/or those which the service allowed the buyer to undertake (e.g. laughing during and after the circus performance).

The machinery ('frozen' previous activity itself) and management actions that went into producing a good were typically 'shared' with many other goods. This is what we call 'scale economies'. Another kind of sharing, based on 'economies of scope', are assuming greater importance as we move from the industrial economy to the co-productive one. With multi-functional micro-processor technology, a given manufacturing system or any other asset can be increasingly used for several purposes, and for different offerings. This changes the micro level of offering architecture, for it allows the obtaining of competitive unit costs without the standardized, large-scale production runs of the industrial economy. Variety takes the place of quantity, but cost and activity sharing is still required.

Another industrial era distinction between 'goods' and 'services' concerns the micro-level difference regarding what happens in a transaction situation. When the activities transferred from supplier to customer are embodied in a physical good, and ownership of the good is transferred, we have traditionally spoken of a product. This is regardless of whether there is much knowledge transferred as 'auxiliary' activities complementing the physical embodiment.

If, on the other hand, most of the transfer of knowledge and activities involved in a commercial transaction entails or is centred upon the activities of people (or 'systems', as in the case of an automatic teller) in a particular place at a given time ('here and now'), rather than being expressed in a physical manifestation, the industrial economy would be referring to a 'service'. Again, this is regardless of whether auxiliary, related, activities are transferred with the service as products.

The purchase of a car is a good illustration of how meaningless this service/product distinction now is. Along with the car itself is sold delivery from the factory to the car dealer, advice, insurance (e.g. warranties), after-sales service, etc. Thus an apparently good-centred transaction also includes a substantial amount of services and, as we have seen, much of the cost of the 'good' is itself made up of service activities: prior research into safety, logistics and quality control services, engineering and design services, etc.

While the ownership of physical manifestations of past activity is still significant in the coproductive economy, gaining *access to use* of offerings (as in the case of car hire) is becoming increasingly important. Thus there are service activities in which most of the knowledge transferred to the customer is embodied in a good, but only access to the good is transferred, not its ownership. Take certain public telephone services: when making a phone call, we do not buy the whole telephone network but simply the right to access it, and we pay for the particular use we make of it. Ownership of the physical products comprising the telephone system remains with the provider.

From this analysis we can infer that many 'service-intensive' offerings exist when no way of 'packaging' human activities into an easily transferable physical embodiment (or 'good') has yet been found. For instance, a medical doctor's knowledge has not, as yet, been 'canned' in expert system computer software for patients to access directly the here-and-now diagnosis and prescription activities performed by the provider.

In the industrial economy, centred on scale economics, services needed to be 'productified' to become economically viable, as with the example of the mutual fund. Access is, as we have suggested above, an alternative to ownership transfer which the scope economics of the emerging service, or co-productive, economy offer. Here offering competitiveness is based not on how much material ownership they transfer but rather on how effectively they render productive resources accessible.

When we referred earlier in this book to the 'liquification' of assets, we attempted to convey how today's technological and social developments are contributing to the accelerated transferability, and thus improved access, to knowledge or activity sets, thereby changing the world map of business. This means in practical, 'micro', terms that new activity configurations replace old ones. Thus, in some situations, 'goods'-centred 'products' are replacing what used to be transacted as services. One can thus listen to music of high sound quality via a compact disc, rather than having to go to a concert hall; banks now have automated teller machines, and there are even automated receptionists in Tokyo office buildings. This tendency, which we have inherited from the industrial economy, is matched by access-providing 'services' replacing the purchase of goods. Leasing cars is an example, so is the outsourcing of facility management, where suppliers maintain (and, if needed, upgrade) buildings or equipment, rather than having each building or equipment owner buy and severely underutilize required support equipment and know-how.

As we stated earlier, all relationships between economic actors are manifested in offerings. An offering engages each economic actor participating in a commercial relationship with others in multiple activities. Offerings organize activities along several dimensions:

(1) *In time*, as they store past activities and simultaneously entail a code for potential future activity;
(2) *In space or location*, geographically grounding the simultaneity of activities characteristic of the current technological era and for the sequentiality of the past; and
(3) *In terms of the relationships among actors* involved in the co-production of value in the offering. It is in this sense that offerings create and define social systems. Offering designers must address the question of how different actors' activities are to be configured for optimum value creation: who does what, when, where, and with whom?

The total activity set which an offering assumes is constantly being 'unbundled' and 'rebundled' in innovative ways, as our McKesson example illustrated. Sub-bundles of the whole are assigned to those actors who are able to peform most efficiently given activities, enabling others to access and use them as effectively as possible. This is done so that the value of the total activity configuration is maximized, making the offering competitive. The total activity in the offering is assigned to the relevant actors by the principles of comparative advantage, which both leads to and is fed by specialization and a consequent division of work. Offerings in this sense can be seen to be 'boundary definers', or 'boundary makers', where the boundary is made up of a multiplicity of actors coming together to create value with and for each other.

14 From value chain to value constellation

Our view of the division of work in value-creating processes clearly differs from the prevailing models which, as we saw earlier, take the 'value chain' as their referent. Instead, our view of the offering as the boundary where actors come together to co-produce value leads us to consider actors coming together in 'value constellations'.

From this more relevant value constellation perspective, value is co-produced by actors who interface with each other. They allocate the tasks involved in value creation among themselves and to others, in time and space, explicitly or implictly. This opens up many opportunities for defining relationships between actors and reassigning activities. If we look at a single relationship in a co-productive system (for example, that between customer and supplier) this view implies that the customer is not only a passive orderer/buyer/user of the offering, but also participates in many other ways in consuming it, for instance in its delivery. Etymologically, consumption means value creation, not value destruction; this sense of consumption is inherent in the 'value constellation' point of view. Furthermore, as actors participate in ways that vary from one offering to the next, and from one customer/supplier relationship to the next, it is not possible to take given characteristics for granted: co-producers constantly reassess each other, and reallocate tasks according to their new views of the comparative advantage they perceive each other to have.

An effective offering is thus designed in such a way so that partners end up performing the 'right' activities for them, engendering value creation on both, or rather *all*, sides. The 'right' activities are those which most successfully match, fit and/or complement the activity sets the partner(s) is/are capable of and willing to perform. This will depend on the partners' available knowledge and resources, and thus on the nature of their value-creation logics, a concept we discuss below.

15 The offering as code carrier

So far, we have defined value in terms of the concentration and availability of resources and activities along a combination of time/location, and actor, dimensions: what, when, where with whom, ... But to further clarify the nature of economic transactions implied in the offering we must introduce another aspect of what value entails.

In addition to the cost of the past or 'supplier' activities, activities which have gone 'into' producing an offering; the value of an offering also reflects what its acquirer can do with it. When customers buy a 'good' or a 'service', they are typically less interested in what went into it than in what it helps them achieve. Some offerings fetch a 'premium price', for their worth to a particular customer is significantly higher than the cost of the activities that went into producing them. For example, if a particular type of corkscrew enables us to uncork a wine bottle without having to use force and without breaking the cork, we are prepared to pay a great deal more for it than the low cost of the materials and activities that went into making it. The inferior or superior value of an offering, below or above the cost of the activities that make it available to us, can be attributed to what we will call the offering's *code.*. This code determines what we call the offering's *leverage* value. The code links the past activities stored in the offering ('frozen' activity flow) and the value-creating activities of customers, and customers' customers, it engenders or enables.

We have seen that effectiveness of an offering is related to how well it 'packages' and makes activities available for a user/consumer within a time/space unit; that is, how it increases the user's options for value creation. An offering carries a code for the value-creating activities it makes possible; that is, it gives users indications about what it allows them to do and what not to do with it, thereby triggering user activities.

The code is, in a sense, the in-built pedagogical element of the offering, and as such influences customer and user behaviour. The value of the offering to the customer will then be dependent on how well the offering code fits the customer's other resources. The extent of this *fit* determines the offering's *leverage value*. Obviously, without an appropriate code, the potential of stored activities 'packaged' in the offering cannot be interpreted and accessed by the customer, so its leverage value will be low or even non-existent.

The offering code is built into the physical embodiment of an offering, as in a machine that requires two buttons to be pressed simultaneously for it to be operated; or it can be embodied in people, such as a doctor saying what he can give medical advice on. It can also be built into systems supporting self-help, such as an '0800' or 'green' free telephone information number or an automatic teller machine; or indeed in combinations of all three.

The offering code may also take several different forms: it can be located in the pricing formula (such as warranties), in the physical design of the good, in the layout of the service environment, in the individual education of customers, in mass communications (such as advertisments), in instruction leaflets, in packaging, etc.

Take a simple, banal product such as a tomato. Virtually everyone knows how a tomato is best eaten and what kinds of recipes can be used to prepare a meal from one. Here the code is contained in experience, in having watched others cook, in cookery books, or in having travelled abroad (did you know that to peel a tomato in countries with polluted irrigation, burning off the peel is the most efficient way of doing so?), and in the tomato itself: is it ripe? rotten?. Compare the code in the tomato to the code in a frozen dish made with tomatoes. Here the customer activities engendered by frozen food is that of choosing the dish in the supermarket (ripeness or rottenness is irrelevant), putting the food in the microwave oven to defrost and heat up *as indicated by instructions* (the code) on the packet.

With some of the more exotic tropical fruits and vegetables which supermarkets sometimes attempt to introduce onto the mass European market, suppliers often accompany their introduction with a certain amount of customer education, an explicit code, say in the form of a brochure or a poster, explaining how the food in question should be prepared and eaten. The customers need to know whether it is sweet or savoury, whether it should be cooked or can be eaten raw, and perhaps what types of recipes can be used. Only then will the offering have value for the customer, unless, as one of the authors did, you go into an oriental shop to buy items with instructions in an unknown language, so as to experiment. This implies a different fit, and thus a different offering and a different value, than that which an experienced oriental buyer of such foods would seek.

The value of the offering is related to the way in which it assigns activities to the different actors involved in the transaction. As we saw previously, all offerings act as attributors of roles: which activities are to be performed by which actors. Every interface between business partners constitutes a 'division of work'. Dividing activities between supplier and customer is an optimization problem, relating to what each partner can do best, fastest, cheapest, most cleanly or whatever (Van der Heijden, 1993). New activity-sharing configurations can take place through making offering codes match better, ensuring that the codes reflect each actor's capacity. This can be done explicitly or implicitly, informally or formally. An example of good matching that was centred exclusively on the right code is the use of the 'Post-it' product developed by 3M; apparently conventional market tests failed to uncover it, but someone realized that its code, when actualized, rendered the invention a hit. Today it is difficult to think of office work without 'Post-it notes'; however, this was not self-evident as no similar code precedent existed: the value of the offering, hidden in the code, awaited the customers discovering it.

If the assembly instructions which IKEA provides with its furniture kits were incomprehensible to its customers, then the code would not make the offering accessible to them, and they would not be mobilized to carry out the activities enabling them to get maximum value out of the offering. In highly co-productive relationships, where suppliers *enable* customers more than they *relieve* them, as is the case with IKEA, the wrong code system will make the offering have virtually no value for the customer, severely hampering the offering's competitiveness.

16 Leverage

Having an offering *code* that enhances fit for potential value-creating activities between supplier and customer is necessary. But this potential fit must be *actually* matched for the customer to obtain value. This is where the concept of *leverage* comes in.

Leverage arises if the offering triggers customer activities which make the customers more effective, thus enabling them to create value in a better way, *whatever 'better' means* for the *customer*. Thus the minimum price of an offering will be typically related to the cost of putting together the activities (or shares thereof) which it stores; the maximum price will be based on the extent to which the offering leverages value creation in the customer.

Effective leverage, that is, in terms of customer use of an offering, is determined not by what a firm achieves in its own business but by what it helps its customer to achieve. One means of leveraging is to look beyond the customer to the customer's customer as a basis for designing the offering, as McKesson did with independent American pharmacies. McKesson's strategy reconfigured both its own value-creation system and those of its customers, suppliers and partners: it leveraged the value-creating activities of all these.

Leverage creates the 'right' opportunities for the customer. It enhances customers' value-creation options by looking at their businesses in new ways. Leverage explores and exploits opportunities based on a better utilization of the joint resources of both parties, as well as those of subcontractors, partners or other suppliers as appropriate.

A company that is 'customer oriented' must be oriented in this advanced 'leverage' sense. As such, it must realize that it cannot rely on asking its customers what it can do for them. Instead, good customer service results from a joint problem-solving process, in which the company tries to integrate both its own knowledge and that of its customers to discover new ways of creating more value through more effective means of matching shared activities.

As we have seen earlier, leveraging can take the form of *relieving* and/or *enabling* the customer. Both concepts concern the configuration of activities as they are manifested in the relationship linking customer and supplier; that is, in the offering. The activities the customers must perform to be most effectively leveraged are made clear to them via the offering code.

Relieving implies assigning activities which the customers used to, or could do, for themselves to the supplier if their comparative advantage so warrants it. As a result of relieving, the resources in the customer's productive system are freed, to be directed to the tasks where the customer has comparative advantage. Much of the explosion of the so-called 'services industry' in its sense of 'tertiarization of the economy' is related to the 'unbundling' and 'outconfiguring', or outsourcing, of activities that are not directly related to the core activities of clients. Cleaning and building maintenance, security guard services, and catering are good examples. The outconfiguring of such activities typically allows clients to focus their attention on producing cars, transporting them (see the example of Ryder System in Part Three for an illustration), providing education or whatever their core activity is. The comparative advantage of the reliever, in the knowledge and resource-sharing relationship, typically comes from specialization and the economies of scale that can thereby be achieved.

Relieving offerings not only take the form of services, as above, but are also very often manifested as 'goods' made available to thousands of clients. Take, for example, Ryder System's view of its role as a transportation company, whose fleet of trucks serves many clients and relieves each of them of building its own transportation fleet. Other offerings relieving customers are goods whose ownership is transferred, for example, an electric drill, which relieves customers of having to make their own drills or having to drill manually, which would take more time and energy.

A relationship between supplier and customer where the offering plays an *enabling* role supports customers in doing things they could otherwise have not done previously or to do these things better. It amounts to configuring activities *in* of even *into* the customer's productive system more effectively. Whereas relieving offerings take activities *out* of the customer system, allowing customers to concentrate on what they do best, enabling offerings support the activities they perform. An example is a Polaroid camera, which enables customers to produce their own photographs, whether on the top of Mount Everest or in the garden at home, without having to hire the services of a professional photographer or film processor.

Note that no offering is 'inherently' a *relieving* or an *enabling* one; these characteristics are a function of how offerings fit into the customer's value creating.

Relieving was arguably the main logic with which offerings in the industrial era worked with customers. Offerings which *enable* attempt to mobilize, build on, stimulate, or install capacities within the client system. The Macintosh desktop publishing system referred to earlier has been a typical enabling offering with a high leverage value: its vast code, with ever-new software packages, built in new types of capabilities and triggered new activities in the customer's system.

There have been many battles between relieving versus enabling philosophies in marketing teams and strategic plans. Doing the one where the other is prevalent seems to pay off, for a while, and is one of the fundamental aspects of successful invasion strategies.[1] As in the classic story of teaching a hungry man to fish instead of giving him a trout, in the financial services industry there have been many battles between those who do things *for* clients and those who *helped* the clients to set up their own in-house operations, such as captive insurance companies or 'in-house banks'.

---

[1]   See Normann (1989) for a more complete analysis of invasion strategies.

17 Value-creation logics

We have shown above that for leveraging to be effective, the value creation it engenders must coincide with customers' *value-creation logics*. With this refocusing of attention from the product to the customer, the company begins to see itself as a support system, someone who is in business because they are able to help the customers to create value and success for themselves and for *their* own customers.

The original product thus becomes the *historical* means by which the supplier's customer base, and therefore the customer's value creation, was accessed. It is from this historical base that *offering* design evolves. The offering seen in this way is not only a 'still' work-sharing formula, but instead a dynamic process. Given the necessary productive knowledge, which can also be accessed or acquired through business partners or other means, and a creative reinterpretation of the customer's value-creation logics, a smart supplier can design more effective co-productive relations with these customers.

We propose that instead of being concerned to identify and fulfil customer *needs*[1] it is more helpful, and strategically more relevant, for a supplier to focus on identifying and offering activities which complement its customer's activity processes. Note

---

[1] We would postulate that the notion of customer needs has limited use in the context of the emerging logics. For some time there has been a debate as to whether needs are real or are artificially created through successful marketing and advertising. What companies offer is supposed to fulfil the 'needs' which customers have. A company's commercial accomplishments are supposed to be a function of how successful the company is in identifying and responding to customer needs. Co-productive business logics make this customer need metaphor less interesting from a strategic point of view. As we have seen above, what matters is that customers encounter support for their own value-creating processes. The focus on 'needs' is thus replaced with one on complementing customers' competences and activities, i.e. on the customers' value creation.

that by 'complementing' we do not mean 'equalling', but rather *fitting in with* customers' activities.

Customers engage in activities to achieve value, not only financial value, but also social, psychological, aesthetic, moral values. Inasmuch as a good supplier is one who helps the customer to create value more effectively, the supplier must be aware that 'more effectively' may entail reduced cost, but much more as well. It may involve increased speed, quality or reliability; superior enjoyment; greater safety; more meaningfulness; or an almost infinite set of other parameters, whose only common denominator is that the customer and, more importantly, the customer's customers, value them. 'Customer' here is not only a commercial counterpart, depending on the type of value the customer is creating, it can include children, spouse, neighbours, or community.

To create value, a customer, who is always also a value creator, needs to be supported with what are traditionally termed 'goods', 'services' and 'information'; that is, with offerings and their associated code. We propose that it is impossible to produce value without the support of any one of these three elements in any situation, and that physical entities, personal or system action, and information are necessary components of all offerings.

One may buy all three elements with the price attached only to one, as is the case when we buy a car with a one-year warranty and a service manual. Yet we need all three elements to derive value from the car. If the car breaks down, the repair service will be essential to allow the customer to continue deriving value from the car. If the instructions manual is not detailed enough to enable the owner to change the tyres when necessary, value creation will again be hampered.

Because value-creation logics vary from one customer to another, it is a key element in the supplier's job to match the value-creating activities of the particular customer group he or she is addressing, case by case. The Sony Walkman 'mobile music system' coincides with the value-creation logics of a customer wishing to listen to music; yet models have been developed for those who want to put the machine in their shirt pockets in the train, or while jogging, or who wish to listen to music while taking a shower, and so on. In all cases, the Walkman enables the customer to listen to music while carrying out other activities simultaneously.

But a Walkman would not, however, enable value creation for someone who would rather listen to high-quality stereo sound on the latest hi-fi system while resting in a comfortable armchair at home, or wanting to listen to Pavarotti live.

Microprocessors are contributing to the increasing diversity of offerings, be they Walkman stereo sets, Nike shoes or vehicle tyres. It does this by allowing scope economics-based variety without having to produce the long production runs of standardized homogeneous outputs, thereby better matching market subsegments. That these are becoming ever narrower is so because it is possible for them to become narrower: microprocessing multifunctionality and scope economics allow the considerable research and development required, and production investments to be recovered all in helping ever better matching to be achieved.

18 Inherent dimensions of offerings[1]

In order to fit in with customers' value-creation logics, offerings must be delivered in the 'right' place, at the 'right' time, in the 'right' form by the 'right' party for each particular customer. Thus, for instance, there is no longer any such thing as a bar of steel: it has to be at the right time in the right place, it has to have the right type of alloys in it and be of the right dimensions, and come with the required technical and information-support systems for it to be of any use to the producer who will use it to create value. With the increasing liquification of assets we have described, the trend is for all offerings to be available just-in-time, any time, any place, no matter, as Stan Davis (1987) put it.

The increasing temporal flexibility which technical constraint breakdown brings about makes it possible to position more precisely offerings in time (and in space). Essentially, this has two effects. One is time *saving*: the reduction of time spent in queues, etc., which frees time for other activities. The other is time *enrichment*: the opportunity to perform several activities simultaneously, increasing the activity density of time/space units, thus making time use more 'effective'. In fact, many firms find that they are no longer competing simply for the customer's money but more and more for the customer's time. The ability to 'create' and to 'save' time, to reconfigure activities in time, is becoming a prerequisite for accessing and keeping customers and customer relations.

The ability physically to disperse and relocate activities where they are most efficiently performed is also becoming a prerequisite

---

[1] For an earlier version of this analysis, see Normann and Ramirez (1989).

for obtaining and keeping value-creating relationships with customers. There is currently a large-scale relocation of activities internationally, which, of course means job transfers. An example is China which is receiving large quantities of foreign investment, and is said to be destined to reach a manufacturing capacity equivalent to half of the world's total over the next 10 years. Take also Swiss Air, whose ticket-processing services were transferred from high-cost Switzerland to low-cost Bombay.

Offerings include 'dimensions' such as *range, time span* and the relative amount of activity *options* the offering allows. Offerings whose range is relatively narrow cover fewer aspects of the customer's value creation than broader offerings. An example of broadening the offering occurred in the case of Volvo's Swedish personal car business in the late 1970s. At this time customer loyalty was diminishing, costs were going up faster than the income of customers in the stagnating Swedish economy, and new models were delayed. Apart from an effort on quality, Volvo engaged in a complete offering turnaround. First, they began to apply the view that they were making money from customers and not cars. A customer who came back to buy another Volvo was more valuable than one who did not, and so it was worth the effort to create such customers. Customers who serviced their cars in the Volvo system and bought original spare parts would generate more business than those who did not, so it was worth thinking about the customer beyond the original sale. Second, it was found that customers were not in the business of buying cars. Most of them were in the business of using cars, creating value in the form of transportation, safety, prestige, identity, while trying to have as much money as possible left for other value creation. It was found that the Volvo cars of the period could be made to satisfy many of the criteria mentioned quite well, the exception being that of leaving a competitive amount of residual available income for customers. Volvo thus began to look wholistically at the car from the user's point of view which led to their 'car ownership economy' concept.

All the cost generators of car ownership were analysed in detail: depreciation, fuel consumption, service, spare parts, taxes, insurance, petrol, and even toll fees. Strategies for dealing with each of these aspects with the purpose of creating better car ownership economy for customers were then designed. Since Volvo cars were considered safer than other cars and Volvo buyers calmer drivers than others, a lower-cost insurance could be argued for. Its cost would, in addition, be lower still if it could be bought in bulk and distributed with the car. A range of clever financial packages was designed, and strategies to influence the second-hand car market and therefore keep depreciation relatively low were outlined. Systems to enable 'do-it-yourself-people' to service their cars on their own and to buy spare parts, even reconditioned second-hand ones, by mail order made it possible for new categories of buyers to drive Volvos. Volvo drivers were given a discount when buying petrol and other products from a certain chain of petrol stations. To identify themselves and to facilitate payment, Volvo owners were offered a special credit card.

What we see here is a change of the offering based on a shift of perspective. Instead of seeing themselves as a company selling cars, Volvo in Sweden now saw themselves as a company supporting the car ownership and utilization of their customers. This shift of perspective meant putting oneself in the customer's shoes and then designing a 'support system' for the customer. In this system the car was, of course, a very essential component, but in fact it can also be seen as the 'entry point' to the customer's value-creation system. This was then a door which allowed the offering to be 'broadened' to include support for more of the customer's own value creation.

Offerings also entail a *time span* aspect or 'dimension' which can be strategically crucial. This 'dimension' refers to the time period over which the co-productive relationship with the customer is meant to last. At one extreme we have what can be termed *'transactional'*, or one-off, no strings attached, offerings. At the other we have very long-term *'relationship'* offerings, where offerings are meant to define a long-term working relationship between customer and provider. In the latter case the practical content of the offering may be more or less 'predefined' or 'open'. A credit/debit card is an example: it specifies a range of options and gives guidelines as to who does what, without indicating the exact activities that will take place. Typical means of creating relationship offerings are pricing formulae such as rewards for continued purchasing (for example, airline mileage or free gifts for loyal and frequent credit card use). The strategic definition of the function an offering is supposed to have regarding each customer will determine its ideal time-span aspects.

The third 'dimension' of an offering concerns how it structures activity option possibilities. In this respect an offering may be *'bundled'* or *'unbundled '*. Take, for example, a package holiday which obliges customers to acquire the whole package even if they intend to use only the flight component. One may otherwise 'unbundle' this offering, where customers can exercise the option of buying the hotel reservation separately from the transport. Another customer buying the holiday through unbundled offerings may buy no transport at all because she is travelling by car with a friend, and yet she will hire a motor boat and a tennis court for the sporting activities she plans to perform. What the customer buys may be virtually the same, but the offering design means that the customer has more or less choice of which components she buys and which components she pays for. Unbundling prevents the extensive cross-subsidization, both of ('internal') offering elements and ('externally') among customers in relation to each other, characterizing many bundled offerings. The transparence that unbundling so obtains is an extremely powerful way of analysing inefficient offering designs, enabling firms to relate to their customers more effectively.

Many aspects of the most successful offerings are so obvious with hindsight that they are almost taken for granted. For instance, take the observation that leverage value depends on how good is the fit between activities carried out by the supplier and the customer. It may be self-evident, but this implies that an offering's leverage value depends very much on how well the location(s) of the offering fit with the action and decision processes in the client system. Because it could act on this factor, General Motor's Acceptance Corporation (GMAC) took very substantial market share from car-financing banks and other lenders. GMAC, as opposed to these other actors, could locate its offering in the car showroom, putting the car and financing decisions in the same place, thereby avoiding much back-and-forth travel to its customers. It thus became the largest consumer lender in the United States.

The 'architecture' of the customer/supplier relationship manifested in the offering in time and space will affect value creation between them. The design of the offering inherently has, explicitly or implicitly, a risk formula included in it as well. This involves aspects such as risk *sharing*, risk *management* and risk *absorption*.

The actors' co-producing value as defined in any offering will be different with regard to:

- Their respective capacity to assess the risks and uncertainties involved;
- Their ability to influence events, and therefore reduce the risks of unpredictable and/or hazardous events occurring;
- Their capabilities to contain, address or absorb the impact of negative consequences should unpredictable, hazardous and/or undesirable events take place;
- Their interest and motivation to address the above elements; and
- Their ability to sustain the more or less temporary negative effects of emergencies.

In offering design it is important to understand that every single offering involves *de facto* a risk-management formula covering all these aspects. This implicit or explicit formula determines how the co-producers share the risks involved in their co-production. Where the risks are considered too difficult or expensive to handle by both parties, additional parties such as insurance companies may be brought in by any one or more to handle specific aspects of those risks. Defining effective risk-sharing formulae may have considerable effects on market behaviour. When Nissan introduced an 'all-costs-guaranteed and included-over-three-years' total risk-reduction package for their Micra car in Sweden in the 1980s (at a price), sales for this car immediately tripled: they found a market niche where existing offerings' risk-management formulae could be successfully redefined. The design parameters of effective risk sharing in offerings such as this typically include unbundling and pricing of separate risks; and/or the stimulation, motivation and rewarding of risk handling or reducing activities.

PART TWO

Value Constellations

Section C   Reconfiguration

19 What is reconfiguration?

New technologies, global competition and changing markets have opened up wider value-creating options, as we have seen earlier. Value has become more 'dense' as we can pack more and more opportunities for value creation into any one offering. The breakdown of physical constraint has allowed for the dispersion or relocation of activities around the world, which is one source of innovative unbundling and rebundling of offering components. Whole value-creating systems are therefore changed, and with them customers' value-creation logics. These changes *'reconfigure'* business relationships, fuelling ways to develop new and existing customer relations and competencies.

As we saw earlier, new technology allows new activity configurations, which become commercially and strategically manifested as new business ideas, as new businesses, and indeed, as new 'industries'. The other side of such processes in action is that existing businesses and industries can become radically redefined, and even extinct. We term this process of activity reallocation among economic actors 'business reconfiguration'. Reconfiguration takes place at three levels:[1]

- *Offerings.* As we have seen above, these comprise what in the industrial economy were termed 'goods', 'services' and 'information'. New offerings imply business development; or business development is made up of offering innovation.
- *Organizations.* Reconfiguration comprises both intra- institutional boundary changes and inter-institutional arrangements. This means that reconfiguration is not only a matter for CEOs and division managers: one can reconfigure one's own department,

---

[1] Cf. Normann (1989) for an earlier discu

or even one's relationship with a single counterpart. Internal and/or external organizational reconfiguration betters the institutional conditions in which offering activity takes place.

- *Mental images or organizing concepts in our minds.* In the end, this concerns the development of an alternative frame of reference, which is the theme of this book.

Offerings are strategically interesting because whatever changes are made to them transform the customer/supplier interfaces which define all organizational boundaries.[2] In the end, it is with the offering and its architecture that business strategies are proven. In order to secure greater income from—and for—customers, it is necessary to make attractive offerings available to them. It is this which will ensure continued positive net income.

Our analysis has led us to conclude that it is offerings, and not firms, that compete in the marketplace for customers. It is offerings, not firms, which fit into customers' value creation and compete with each other for their money. The money is the value 'residue' making up the difference which remains between the activities carried out by the supplier and those by the customer in co-productive relationships. Firms both compete and collaborate to achieve value-creating offerings. But in all emerging economy marketplaces, be it the 'goods' and 'services' market, the labour market, or the stock market, it is the offering, and not the firm, that is the key unit of analysis in marketplace competition.

The logical link between (1) strategic decision, (2) organizational structure and process and (3) offering design is weak in many business institutions. As offerings are the 'acid test' of a strategic decision, many companies do not have the necessary feedback loops to link changes in (1) and (2) with those in (3) allowing them to monitor the causal effects simply, rapidly and effectively. Computerized technologies such as CAD-CAM, integrated planning/production/marketing infrastructures, concurrent engineering or distributed processing enabling scope economies, shorter design to market delays, and shorter product

---

[2] We accept the concept of 'internal' customers in our reconfiguration world view; but this implies that as 'customers' in markets, 'customers' in firms will have a *choice* of suppliers. Speaking of internal customers thus logically presupposes allowing for outsourcing to effectively compete with existing internal sources.

life cycles must be allowed to overcome the cumbersome organizational (2) processes of yesterday, which often do not favour effective feedback. Those firms who manage to integrate the new business logics by linking (1) and (3) through effective (2) structures and processes are those that achieve the winning reconfigurations. Those that do not are reconfigured by the former. This, then, is the stark choice of the emerging economy: reconfigure or be reconfigured.

It is at the *mental image level* that reconfiguration possibilities emerge or fail to emerge. It is the views in the minds of business people that are the greatest constraint, and the source of greatest opportunities, in business today. New offering designs and organizational possibilities envisioned through our reconfiguration framework at this level mean that there are no 'mature' businesses. There are only 'mature' frames of reference.

The frame is the lens through which managers see the situation with which they are confronted. The framework helps them to 'read' the situation meaningfully, to see its dangers and opportunities, and thereby to act upon it. In order to comprehend the business logics of our time, and act effectively, it is crucial to develop a new mind frame and abandon the old one.

Management's conceptual frameworks rest on metaphors to convey frequently recurring concepts in the organization of business.[3] However, metaphors cease to be adequate when the conditions to which they are applied evolve. So far in this book we have shown how social and technical changes are making the world of business change in radical, fundamental ways which depart from the value-creation logics of the past. These radical changes require new means of designating our conceptual world of management. Using the old metaphors on the new realities implies that there is a gap, which is a dangerous gap of irrelevant, obsolete, misguided thinking—and thus of ineffective business acting. New metaphors which better fit the emerging logics of business are called for. These metaphors will guide business thinking and action to better fit together comparative advantages. They will guide successful commercial innovation. It is this reconfigurative need which this book seeks to address.

---

[3] See Morgan (1986), for a full treatment of this approach.

With the new frame centred on new metaphors, a new conceptual language with which to describe economic phenomena emerges. It includes words such as 'offerings', 'density', 'liquidity' and 'reconfiguration'. The extent to which many managers' views are bound, or even 'yoked', to the value chain concept underlines how constraining old frameworks are. Just as the 'round earth' view of our planet is not a sum of 'flat earth' views, so our proposed 'value constellation' world-view cannot be reduced to adding up interconnected value chains. It requires a conceptual quantum leap to take up the invitation to use the 'escape hatch' (cf. Hama, 1993), the new thinking, which this book presents. From the new point of view we offer, the 'value chain' links among economic actors are seen to be a special case which is helpful in limited circumstances. But you cannot see the new framework by staying with the old frame: one must change one's eyeglasses.

20 Why reconfigure?

Articulating changing business logics

Interfaces between economic actors in relatively stable conditions do not call for frequent reconfiguration. Such conditions typically imply product-oriented business definitions. But from time to time, conditions within value-creation systems change, and/or invaders change the rules of the game (Normann, 1989). Here possibilities for new interface definitions are introduced, and value-creation systems are reconfigured accordingly. This provides a link with the introductory part of this book: quantum leaps in value-creation systems are often related to infrastructure and/or technological changes. Revolutions such as these leave companies who do not question the definition of interfaces, who do not rethink the optimal division of work with other actors, far behind in the competitive race. With such changes becoming common, companies can no longer consider established organizations as clearly defined, separate entities that do not need questioning. Increasingly complex inter-organizational relationships now force them to reconsider their organizational structures and processes, and managing across boundaries is becoming a critical skill (cf. Hirschhorn and Gilmore, 1992).

Viewing customer/supplier interfaces as co-productive relationships, manifested as offerings, in a wider and theoretically unlimited value constellation is a useful way to enable firms dynamically and continually to question, redefine, and reconfigure interfaces. It is the best way to remain competitive in the emerging economy.

In addition, as we see in Part Three particularly when reviewing the Générale des Eaux, the Lyonnaise des Eaux-Dumez, and the Ryder System examples, reconfiguration is a sort of *meta-competence* which allows a firm to match competence development with customer relationship development. By 'meta-competence' we mean a competence of a higher logical typing, that is, which encompasses the core competencies of the lower logical type that make up a company's know-how, know-what and know-who. The 'meta-competence' is a 'know-why'; it entails the business philosophy. This may be known by competitors, but is very difficult indeed to copy. It relates to what Selznick (1957) called 'distinctive competence', which is the *systemic* competence that integrates other competencies into a coherent business practice. Reconfiguring is such a *meta-competence*, arguably the most strategically crucial one in the emerging economy, where you either reconfigure or are reconfigured by others.

Competition : the battle for customer bases

Customers in the emerging economy attain a strategic significance far beyond that which traditional micro-economic theory attributes to them. Taken within our co-productive framework, they are active partners in the joint value-creation process, not simple passive recipients of the value creation of others. Both they and the relationships firms have with them are, from this viewpoint, crucial assets in their own right. As with all acquired assets, investments in customer relations must be managed and a return on investment secured if the capital is to be preserved and nurtured. Never mind that traditional accounting methods ignore or undervalue this asset, even if it is not in the balance sheet it may be one of the most crucial assets in the long run.[1]

The increasing concern with quality which firms have experienced in recent years is an important sign that customers have become more capable of abandoning commercial relationships that prove unreliable and inconsistent. Companies have therefore been forced to change their priorities. In addition to decreasing product design, production or personnel costs, it has also become

---

[1]   For a developed version of this argument, see af Petersens and Bjurström, (1991).

necessary to take steps to avoid the loss of income resulting from enlightened customers switching suppliers or demanding costly corrective measures. It has become crucial to begin calculating costs and revenue as manifested first and foremost in the customer's value creation rather than at one's own factory. This, rather than production costs, is now the basis of economic calculations.

IKEA, which we review in some detail in Part Three, of the book, has a philosophy of being the lowest-priced supplier in its markets: the rest of the organization is configured with this 'baseline' as the grounding principle. By reversing the established way in which the grounding 'baseline' is established, making the customer rather than production define this 'baseline', IKEA has grown into the world's largest retailer of home furnishings.

Jan Carlzon, the CEO of Scandinavian Airlines System (SAS) during the 1980s, when customer relations became critical, once said, 'A satisfied customer is our most valuable asset'. This reflected the far-reaching change process he piloted. Rank Xerox in Germany in 1993 reportedly indicated that its priorities, in order of importance, were (1) customer satisfaction, (2) employee satisfaction, (3) market-share growth, and (4) profitability. This did not mean that it was willing to be unprofitable; it did mean that it was willing to sacrifice some shorter-term profitability to grow the now more crucial assets for longer-term success.

Acquisitions are often made at prices that seem unjustified from the perspective of traditional asset value calculation. At a closer look, it becomes clear that they were seen as a means of accessing new customer bases. Take, for example, the sale of Eastern Airlines' shuttle service in the highly competitive market in and out of La Guardia airport in New York. Once a first price for the transaction had been negotiated, a strike took place and the service came to a standstill. The price was subsequently lowered by an amount equivalent to the value of three Airbus aircraft. We interpret this price reduction to the resulting customer dissatisfaction-led decreased value of the customer base.

Given the increasing importance of customers as assets, one of the most crucial questions to be addressed when making business decisions is how these assets are being taken care of; how well their potential is being utilized; and who is responsible for both. Below we investigate the customer base as an asset from three viewpoints:

(1) How customer base stakes are becoming both larger and more volatile, relative to traditional assets.

(2) How management systems and our strategic framework fit to best monitor the profitability (business result) that customers generate.

(3) How, in the final analysis, firms do not make money from customers (or, of course, their products!) but from their customers' value-creation activities.

There are a number of reasons established relationships with customers can no longer be taken for granted. First and foremost, the customer is becoming more active, educated and sophisticated. When acting as customers individuals are becoming much more discriminating. Easily accessible information and better education, a sharper sense of identity, changing values on how time and resources are spent makes customers more 'difficult', more 'choosy and picky'. They do not want to waste their time, or have suppliers waste it or steal it from them. They want to save and/or to enrich their time. They want their spending and consumption to fit with and enhance their lifestyles and identities. As many surveys show, they increasingly want to be viewed as individual human beings, not as 'cases', 'patients', or 'accounts', and treated with respect and consideration. Distinction and recognition are trends, moving away from being viewed as an impersonal 'average' client who does not exist in practice.

This evolution in individual customer sophistication can be related to the evolution of business customers: they, too, are becoming more demanding, more discriminating, better informed. They, too, have experienced a widening of the choices available to them, and a willingness to exercise them. They are driven by the way in which their business problems and business options develop, which in turn reflects the wider reconfiguration options that are becoming available to their own customers as well as to their suppliers. Business customers are also forced to rapidly integrate and realign with new technologies and the possibilities they offer.

When we analysed the customer base of a large and successful European retail bank, with a particularly strong position among large corporate customers, we found signs of deep change in the customers which had not been noticed by the bank. Traditionally, capital scarcity and currency regulations constraints had rendered the companies which were the bank's clients very dependent on banks for access to capital to finance their growth, their invest-ments in new manufacturing technology, and their acquisitions. Long-term credits established the core offering architecture of the ongoing relationship between the bank and its customers. In return for such loans customers were loyal to the bank when buying other services, and the banks were generous in providing 'free', or bundled, advice and contacts for initiatives such as international acquisitions.

But over a period of a few years the business situation had changed drastically. Regulation had been liberalized, foreign competition became important, and margins diminished. New markets, new sources of equity and new ways of accessing other capital had become available. The finance director of a large corporation could expect ten or twenty telephone calls a day from banks around the world offering their services, usually un-bundled. Many of the large corporations set up 'internal banks' taking over many of the former functions offered by the banks, including cash management and capital market operations. Some of them, like General Electric and ABB, had even started to sell these services to other external companies, thereby competing with the banks.

The bank we were working with found itself in a dilemma. The traditional long-term loan, basically a simple product based on tradition and regulation, became both less profitable than before and less dependable in maintaining the customer relationship. Customers were shopping around more, and were looking at banks to provide selective expertise, often on a rather short-term basis, in connection with deals and other kinds of restructuring. Long-term 'relationships' requiring few and simple competencies gave way to many short-term, knowledge-intensive transactions requiring rapid responses, and the tailoring of a multitude of competencies for the occasion. Unbundling of the previously bundled co-production revolutionized the relationship, and changed the logic of how to invest in customer assets. This forced this bank to fundamentally reconsider its *meta-competence*, its way of tying in customer evolution and competence evolution in com-petitive offerings. In many ways, the business it considered itself to be in was revolutionized, with new priorities replacing old ones, with old know-how displaced by new knowledge, changing the way it built and kept relations with customers.

The growing volatility of customers is accompanied by productivity gains in stagnant or shrinking markets, particularly for companies operating in Western countries with decreasing birth rates. This increases the relative scarcity of customers. In turn this is shaping many business strategy competitive battles. As the total number of potential customer relationships diminishes, the stake in each and every one of the remaining relationships naturally becomes higher.

While the competitive battle today is therefore centred on positioning the firm to occupy a sufficiently large role in supporting the customer's value creation, this does not automatically mean broadening the offering. SAS, for example, after making an expensive strategic mistake centred on broadening its air travel offering to business travellers, as it was erroneously thinking that it could also offer them world-wide hotel accommodation, chose after to provide passengers with a 'do not disturb me' sign they can use when travelling on a plane. Thus, after the change its passengers were in a position to decline options if they so wish.

The move from simple, one-way, sequential, transactional business logics towards co-productive, reciprocal, synchronous, relational ones is both a result of and a contribution to the increased stake in customer relationships. As the interface between company and customer becomes more complex, and more volatile at the same time, it also requires more attention and more mental as well as physical investment. In practical terms, companies are becoming organized to reflect customers; be it as segments or even as individual value creators, as witnessed by the evolution of 'personal bankers' and 'key account managers'. Firms must also invest in developing relationships with partners, subcontractors, alliances, joint ventures, franchise arrangements, etc. in order to acquire the necessary competences and resources to produce value for and with their customers. These mental and physical investments then put pressure on increasing the return on them.

The second view of customer bases as assets concerns customer profitability. In long-term relationships, it is important to ensure that customers are profitable both for the firm and for themselves.

As a Federal Express advertisement put it in the late 1980s 'If you don't take care of your customers somebody else will'.

The battle for customer loyalty can thus be taken a step further. First, it is necessary for firms to think in terms of retaining and using effectively the productive resources inherent in every customer, an asset which has been created or acquired at a cost. Second, the customer should give rise to a sufficient level of price-carrying activities for the firm. Thus a business dynamically marries productive knowledge and customer bases with a view to generating profitability for both parties. While it is true that unless a firm has satisfied customers it will not be in business if there is competition, it is also a fundamental and all-too-common fallacy to reverse the argument and to assume that satisfied customers will create a profitable business. In fact it is necessary to monitor *both* customer satisfaction *and* customer profitability.

Economics teaches us that we should look at the return we get from our scarce resources. We have learnt to consider return on capital or return on equity. If customers are becoming an increasingly critical resource, it follows from economic theory that we should look at the return we get on them. Companies typically have developed sophisticated methods to calculate return on capital, profitability per product, profitability per factory, profitability per product or product line, etc. But what about customers?

Consider the following results taken from customer base analyses carried out by the authors' consulting practice:

- In a manufacturing company, about 40% of its individual customers were unprofitable; the two largest customers by sales volume were among the three most unprofitable ones; and the very largest customer (in terms of its own turnover) was also by far the most unprofitable, generating large losses.
- In a large European continental bank, 74% of the private customers (not counting a small segment of 'VIP' customers) were unprofitable, and generated a loss equal to three times the profit of the retail banking operations. The remaining 26% of the customers contributed the total profit, plus twice the total profit to cover the losses generated by the other customers.
- In one company, 10% of the customers represented 180% of the total profit.

- The profit margin per customer varied between plus 65% and minus 179% in one company.

There are many reasons for the above results. In the era when companies started to calculate profit by small production unit, or by product, similar results and surprises were frequently encountered. The overall conclusion common to the above examples is that no-one had paid attention to the issue of customer profitability.

On a more detailed level, an important answer available to firms facing such issues is to shift cost structures, particularly through redefining the established relationship between costs counted as 'direct' and those as 'indirect'. Most companies have assumed that it is enough to sell products whose profitability they know and control. But in fact our studies show that while revenues from customers tend to come from sales of goods and services (offerings), the cost side of the relationship is much more complex. Customers induce costs which are not only product-related but are also related to the number of orders, to the size of each order, to how they relate with the supplier, to the special attention (typically, not invoiced) that a supplier pays to a given customer, to the special resources that a supplier 'exceptionally' devotes to a particular customer (time and again), and, in general, to the individual customer's substantial skill and propensity to draw on a supplier's resources.

We have to distinguish clearly between what constitutes the offering and to what the price tag is attached. As we have seen above, it is not only possible, but also usual, for customers and invaders to 'unbundle' the offering. When customers do this in ways that render them unprofitable, they buy few price-carrying elements and many elements that do not carry a price.

We analyse this by looking at some examples. In most countries, banks have put a price on deposit and lending services, providing other services 'for free'. For example, the cost to the customer of having one or four different accounts has been largely the same, though the cost to the bank has certainly been related to the number of accounts. Transactions typically have been free in most countries: a customer writing ten cheques per week, at a realistic real cost to the bank of, say, $2, has been charged more or less the same (i.e. zero) as the customer writing no cheques. As a result, different customers have developed greatly varying 'consumption styles' creating unnoticed but in reality extremely varying costs for the supplier.

In many industries customers have discovered this possibility, and have developed the art of 'cherry picking' to a high level of refinement. This is possible as companies themselves have not calculated what activities they devote on a customer basis, only on a product or product line basis.

Looking at the customer as the source of profitable business requires a change of mental map. We can think of the business potential of a customer along two dimensions. One, highlighted by the focus on 'quality' and customer loyalty, is our old friend, the time dimension. If we can get the customer to come back and buy from us time and time again, we will obviously retain more of that customer's business, having a better chance of benefiting from the business potential of a customer relationship. The second dimension is related to the range of offerings that the *customer* buys from a given supplier ('us') as compared with others. By expanding the offering to include elements that match the customer's value-creation logics better than competitors can, we are more likely to capture more of the customer's business; but only if he or she lets us, as SAS in the above example learnt at its expense. This second dimension has attracted a great deal of attention by companies recently, as we can see from the many attempts at 'cross-selling' and 'encircling' in which companies indulge.

To summarize, the business potential of a customer is represented geometrically by the area defined by the *time* and *range* dimensions of the offering. The profit potential of a customer for an individual supplier is determined by the business potential and the offerings (including the pricing formula for these) that a customer buys. It is the offering design that determines which costs a customer will represent in its behaviour for a company. The business and profit potential of a customer base is equivalent to the sum of the potential of each individual customer, plus resulting scale and scope economies which increases may allow for.

A third view of customers as assets considers the customer's success as a condition of the 'supplying' firm's success. In other words, the firm's results will be related to what it helps its customers to achieve, that is, the leverage value of its offerings. This can create a plus-sum game, where suppliers and customers both win as a result of their effective, co-productive, value creation. This in turn depends on how good a fit between the firm's competences and the value-creation logics of the customer. Thus, it becomes evident that firms make money not from satisfying customer needs but from effectively leveraging their value creation. Firms generate revenue by creatively shaping and inputting their productive knowledge, and productive knowledge they can obtain from their own suppliers and partners, at the disposal of their clients so as to match and leverage their own value creation.

A good illustration of ensuring one's own success through ensuring customer success is the case[2] of Baxter Health Care Corporation. Since acquiring its rival, American Hospital Supply, in 1985 Baxter became the largest purveyor of hospital supplies in the United States. In 1994, it was able to supply hospitals with up to 70% of what they utilize to carry out their value creation.

Originally, Baxter's strategy was based on the knowledge it possessed. It consisted in developing a strong 'basic' R&D base in important areas such as blood plasma and kidneys that could then be transformed into applications such as intravenous systems and kidney dialysis machines. However, more recently such knowledge-based strategic developments have been guided by a customer-driven strategic orientation.

The acquisition of its larger competitor, American Hospital Supply, allowed Baxter to gain critical size in its core businesses. It can thus now offer its most important clients, mostly large US hospitals, high quality and low cost. Baxter's strategy 'exploits' the way DRG (Diagnostic Related Group) re-regulation affected its business. DRG, which was introduced by the Reagan administration, basically reshuffled the scarcest resource hierarchy, making Baxter's customers' customers (i.e. patients) relatively scarcer, and thus more valuable assets. DRG re-regulation made operating cost reduction the priority for hospitals, for the cost-plus basis

---

[2] This case concerns a time period closed in 1994. Since then, a major change occurred: Baxter sold its health-care product and cost-management business. In 1996, Baxter spined off Allegiance Corporation, America's leading provider of health-care products and cost-management services. Baxter renews today its focus on its core technologies of renal technologies of renal technology, biotechnology, cardiovascular medicine and medication delivery, and increases its emphasis on global expansion.

upon which they had been operating disappeared. With this, the utilization rate dropped to about 60–64% of capacity.

Baxter offers both 'relieving' and 'enabling' support to its clients' value-creating activities. It has demonstrated skill at judiciously deciding when and where to relieve and where to enable. Baxter does so by collaborating with its clients to understand the potential comparative advantage of each unit: the customer's, its own, its suppliers', and that of the customer's clients. It has developed one of the best-thought-out systems to influence the behaviour of providers, providers' providers, customers, and customers' customers that we know.

Thus, Baxter relieves its customers from doing some things in which it has relative advantage, typically based upon relative scale/scope economies. An example is the initiative it undertook jointly with a pharmaceuticals manufacturer provider to develop pre-mixed intravenous drugs. In so doing Baxter relieved each individual hospital customer from (1) having its own relevant high-cost/low-volume pharmacy operations, (2) stocking and updating the limited-shelf-life components, (3) doing the compounding in house, and (4) controlling quality. All these four costly activities in individual hospitals are now done by Baxter and its supplier for the hospitals at a fraction of the cost. This is a very telling example of brilliant reconfiguration and of consequent offering redesign.

Baxter Health Care also *enables* its hospital clients, enabling them better to relieve and enable their own clients' (i.e. the patients') value creation. An example of enabling is the support which Baxter gives to hospitals providing patients with home health care. These offerings enable hospitals to help their patients, and their families, to help themselves. Baxter devised a system where it, its hospital customers and other suppliers (such as home-delivery firms) can provide recently discharged patients with 24-hour emergency advice by phone, on-call nurses, day visits, information on how to administer medication, regular medication delivery to the home, and transportation to/from the home to the hospital for outpatient visits. This makes, for instance, post-operative care possible at high levels of quality for a fraction of the cost of staying in hospitals, which typically have operating costs that are similar to those of 5-star hotels, if we take the 'filled bed' as a unit of analysis.

Baxter offerings are targeted at various clearly defined 'strategic levels' in its customer system. Thus, Baxter offers support which: (1) goes directly into the patient's body, such as intravenous drugs, which act directly on the patient's own value creation (healing). Then (2) Baxter offerings also directly give help for patient-support actions by others, as, for example, in the case of surgical gloves, which allow the hospital staff's activities supporting the patient. In the same way, (3) Baxter provides support on how this staff is managed by yet others further removed from the patient with its supplying hospital administration.

Distinguishing between the 'strategic levels' at which each targeted value-creation activity is located in the customer value-creation system in this way is useful in 'designing' offering systems that best support customers' value-creating activities. Each 'level' can be understood to effectively 'leverage', or support, the 'next' level's value creation. Because Baxter understands how to exploit this concept of 'strategic levels' in practice, it has avoided making a mistake which companies working on 'value chain' terms have made too often. Thus, Baxter supports its patient-centred value-creation activities at many levels, but has avoided bypassing the hospital. This is very astute, not only because Baxter evidently understands the difference between relative advantage-based strategies and 'vertical integration', but also because in so doing it effectively acquires a return on customer (loyalty) investment at all levels. This would be difficult to obtain through alternative means.

Baxter's understanding of the risk-sharing elements in offerings is also worth noting. This understanding appears related to its being able to see its business from its clients' point of view. It thus placed manufacturing facilities all over the world, enabling hospitals in other countries to buy 'domestic' offerings. An additional advantage for Baxter by placing manufacturing facilities abroad was that its 'captive' distributors could not 'unbundle' Baxter's range of offerings. Instead they had to buy and sell virtually everything (the local) Baxter made. In this way Baxter obtained a measure of customer base access control abroad that many other foreign companies could not secure.

Baxter's capacity judiciously to determine relative advantages between itself and its various actual and potential counterparts has led to innovative cross-industry co-production. An example is the collaboration it developed with Sharp Electronics to make intravenous solution pumps. Our analysis leads us to conclude that Baxter is effectively attempting to become something of an 'infrastructure' for its clients' value creating: healing. Its understanding of actual and potential interactive co-productive relationships with counterparts led Baxter's CEO to state that not only did they create the 'infrastructure' for the home care business in the USA, they actually created the home care 'market' itself.

Baxter's relative lateness in enabling hospitals to improve their own management is perhaps an illustration of the difficulty involved in going from a relieving to an enabling role, from being a 'supplier' to becoming a 'consultant'. This is one aspect of the difficulties IBM faced in the transition from the 1980s to the 1990s. Baxter's merger with AHS, however, seems to have made it possible to make up for this relative lateness. AHS's electronic order and distribution system, the equivalent to hospitals of McKesson's systems for independent pharmacies, enhanced Baxter's relative lags in this area. The similarity with McKesson in Baxter's 'corporate' programme, which serves multi-hospital clients, is striking. Like McKesson's offer, financial and risk-management elements are prominent in the offering design. Baxter includes guaranteed price ceilings and cash bonuses for reaching specified volume purchase targets. Such offering elements help Baxter to keep about 600 hospitals, or roughly one out of every nine hospital beds in the United States, as customers.

Baxter's treatment of hospitals can be compared with McKesson's treatment of pharmacies. Both make it possible for their clients to compete effectively. The enhanced clients' success has ensured that both companies stay in business.

21 Examples of reconfiguration

Offering designs utilizing new technology, and a superior understanding of how customers prefer to allocate time, makes innovative business ideas possible. Sometimes they even create new types of business. The following examples briefly illustrate some offering designs that are in fact only the tip of the iceberg of the reconfiguration that has been taking place in business recently.

Take, for instance, the case of the bio-analyser produced by the French firm, Kis, which defined itself as being the leading company world-wide in the 'instant/real time service' industry. The bio-analyser developed by Kis is meant to be located in a doctor's office, providing instant analyses of organic samples. In the past these were processed in a medical laboratory. The patient and doctor thus save time, and can immediately decide on what action to take to address the identified physiological condition. The bio-analyser reconfigures the activity sets of customers and doctors, eliminating the role of the laboratory for some operations, and bringing in Kis as producer, advisor and service provider to the doctor/customer interface.

The same is true of the portable computer with a built-in fax machine. The user saves time by not having to print, then transfering a printed version of what the user has typed onto the computer to the fax machine. With the programmable fax option, messages can be sent at any time (including after working hours, when rates are cheaper), anywhere, without referring to the other actors and/or machines. The whole process of sending messages is packaged in a single box within reach of the end users, and the fax machine's role, together with the peripheral services (such as maintenance) associated with it, are eliminated.

Note, however, that while these reconfigurations affect whole actor constellations, offerings of this kind do not entirely replace existing arrangements for all customers. Complex or specialized diagnoses are still carried out in laboratories; and many firms still require the services of a fax machine to send large quantities of pre-existing documents.

Matching activity logics better than established actors 'resting on their laurels' is a typical successful invader strategy. Consider American Express, a company which originally started in travel services. In 1990 *Business Week* classed American Express as the US financial services company with the highest market value. Its business may today be regarded primarily as a financial services company, a business with which it has grown in conjunction, but in a distinct way from its travel-related services operations. As a financial services company, American Express is an invader of banks and other established actors in this field. This provides us with some fascinating insights.

American Express's competitors, such as retail banks, have seen themselves and have been seen by others as providers of financial services. They have accordingly been protected by relevant regulations. American Express originally had no such view, and was not so viewed by others. It was not regulated in the same way. American Express saw itself as a provider of services for travellers. Its travellers are increasingly those who spend considerable amounts when travelling. So American Express has built knowledge of customer travel habits as well systems to facilitate and leverage travel and the expenses it generates. Much, but not all, of this system provides financial services. The conclusion might then be that American Express successfully invaded financial services because it matched customer value-creation processes more effectively than traditional suppliers of financial services. The invasion is based on understanding customer value creation, rather than on offering products it happened to have. In other words, in attending to the value-creation processes of a selected group of customers it matches activity logics which were formerly supported by other actors, and does so better than those others.

We have stated earlier that invaders manifest some of the weaknesses or 'blind angles' which established actors have developed with regards to reconfiguration possibilities (Normann,

1989). Without such built-in blind angles, there would be no room for invaders in the first place! An invading supplier often enters the customer's decision-making process at a different strategic level from that with which established actors interface, and thereby sets new rules by which other actors must play.

An example is the loss of territory to invaders suffered by Giant Corporation[1], a firm which manufactures and sells heavy equipment used by different kinds of industrial buyers. A single customer typically buys several items of equipment, which often represents a sizeable investment. The effective utilization of the equipment requires a certain level of specialized knowledge and management capability.

The world market for the equipment is divided between about ten major players, and Giant is one of the most important of these. Each of the players typically sells through franchised but independent distributors who tend to control most of the customer relationships and who also service the equipment.

In the 1980s, with more and more of its customers becoming concerned with their cash management and with the increasing trend towards the subcontracting of services, Giant Corporation gradually became the target of a new type of competition. Companies from the leasing sector began to buy equipment from Giant (and from Giant's established competitors) and then lease it, long and short term, to customers. Some of these leasing companies also developed additional services: the leasing of associated equipment, designing service contracts for the equipment, building service centres which were in competition with those of Giant's dealers, encouraging the evolution of less expensive 'pirate' spare parts, selling education to operators of the equipment, and taking total management contracts for operating it. These leasing companies in fact did everything except move into manufacturing, and since the market for this type of equipment grew in the 1980s, Giant and their competitors enjoyed increasing production and sales figures.

However, centred on expanding their production capability as they were to meet growing demand volumes, they hardly noticed when the value-creation processes of their customers were invaded.

---

[1]   This case concerns a time period closed in 1994.

The competitive game changed so much that the whole industry was redefined. But Giant traditionally defined its industry in terms of their products, and not as their position in their customers' value-creation processes. This was the built-in 'blind angle' exploited by the invaders.

When, finally, Giant Corporation came to analyse the situation in one country where historically they had a strong position, they found the following situation through looking at the sum total of the equipment they had sold in the preceding year:

- About 60% of the Giant machines had been sold as a component of contract agreements rather than in the established way.
- About 35% of the spare parts used for Giant machines were from 'pirate' manufacturers other than Giant.
- About 80% of the service provided to Giant machines were from providers not forming part of Giant's contracted service network.
- Less than 10% of the financing of purchase or lease of Giant machines had been provided by Giant and its contracted network.
- It was also estimated that a number of related auxiliary products and services used in connection with Giant machines were now dominated by and subcontracted through the new breed of competitor. This had happened as Giant had never systematically tried to move into that part of the business, for it was 'peripheral' to its product-centred view. Growing parts of this area of customers' value systems included information control systems and consulting services for designing manufacturing and logistics systems; activities that were in fact taking an increasingly central role in structuring the customer's value creation.

Depending on how we view these developments, we may or may not see a radical change. According to the traditional, product-centred view of the industry, things went well, since Giant's manufacturing and product sales had gone up, and it had even gained market share from its traditional competitors. But if we think about the competitive market as a value-creation constellation, a radically different interpretation may be offered. In its own customer base (defined here as those who utilize a Giant machine), Giant misses out on one-third of the spare parts market, 80% of the 'after-sales' service market (usually the source of over 50% of net profit), and almost all of the financing market. None of these areas can be seen, from our viewpoint, as really comprising a different 'market'. Financing, after-sales service and spare parts are all necessary complementary elements *for the customer*, and in fact constitute an important part of the 'minimum offering' from the customer's point of view, as they enable it to create value as much as Giant's 'core' products.

As Giant began to lose a hold on its understanding of the evolving possibilities in their interface with their customers, they began to realize that even the core component was potentially in danger. The invaders had begun to play off the manufacturers against each other, and this would lead to lower margins as soon as the market boom was over. Customer relationships started to change. Because of the nature of their offering, the invaders had begun to make the financial officers in the client system their customers, whereas brand loyalty to manufacturers like Giant tended to be with client factory managers. In fact, the new competitors had started to redefine the whole purchasing decision. The customer/supplier relationship became less and less a question of what brand of equipment to have (and how many) and increasingly one of defining manufacturing and logistics strategy. Giant's salespeople were very product-oriented (many of them had been operators of such equipment), and they were not able to lead a discussion centering on a manufacturing strategy and its financial and equipment implications. True, Giant still sold their machines. But these machines were now part of an entirely different value-creation process: Giant had been reconfigured.

Other invaders use technology-based time/space reconfigurations in order to take the ball from the courts of other actors and change the system of roles and relationships. Whether or not an invader designs a successful offering, i.e. is capable of entering a customer's value-creation process with it, depends on how well the invading offering can contribute to the value creation of the customer.

Sometimes an offering which is unique simply for its flexibility and in terms of its time/space dimensions may do the job. Such innovations free the customer in time and location from traditional constraints in time and space. The Sony Walkman, the mobile telephone, the personal computer or shopping via Minitel are typical examples of offerings which free the customer from such time/space restrictions.

Such reconfigurations appeal to customers seeking made-to-measure solutions which *enable* the customer to engage in self-service activities. Take, for instance, desktop publishing, which exploits an innovative understanding of customers' value-creation logics. It is at the heart of considerable cross-industry reconfiguring. By enabling customers to be their own graphic designers and to produce quality illustrated documents they would have otherwise been unable to do themselves, Apple, which led the innovation originally, redefined the activities of independent professional customers, as well as that of many publishers, typists, editors, layout artists, direct mail firms, printing houses, and advertising firms. New extensions such as scanning equipment and the possibility of linking directly with lithographic equipment, video and audio equipment further the original wave of reconfiguration.

French customers can in the same way now use their Minitel to consult their bank statement, leave messages for friends and business partners, obtain information on train and air timetables and make their travel reservations, rent an apartment, check companies' credit ratings, verify road conditions, and much more. This means that the activity sets of the actors traditionally concerned with the supply of such services have been reconfigured, leaving control with the customer, who benefits from greater flexibility.

Reconfigurations' unbundling and rebundling activities exploit available resources more effectively in a co-productive relationship. EF Colleges grew into one of the world's largest language-course providers by activating under-utilized resources such as empty schools and vacationing teachers, and combining them with vacationing students and parents wishing to travel abroad.

In competitive markets with dynamic business development, activity sets are being unbundled and rebundled in a more or less continuous process, albeit according to logics which themselves may change radically. Invaders break up productive systems and reintegrate them in new formations and combinations, sometimes with new components, sometimes with old ones, and sometimes by simply reorganizing existing components.

One striking example of such innovation is offered by Oslo Banken, a Norwegian bank established in 1984[2], following the

---

[2] This case concerns a time period closed in 1994. Oslo Banken did not survive. Yet, it did play an important role in dramatically changing the face of the banking industry. As an indication of this, one can identify today followers in other countries — like Mediolanum in Italy, or Skandiabanken in Sweden.

enactment of deregulation measures. Oslo Banken entered banking with a single branch that offered telephone and mail banking services, an idea that Cortal in France and innovators in other countries also utilized. Oslo Banken offered to pay two percentage points more than the competition on deposit rates, and provided loans at the going market rate. Otherwise, Oslo Banken essentially provided only one service: cheque accounts, but customers were charged for each transaction.

The strategy adopted by Oslo Banken was to exploit a 'blind angle'—built-in weakness of traditional banks. Here (priced) deposit banking and lending services are normally bundled together with (free) payment services. By unbundling payment services from deposit services, Oslo Banken could attract customers whose deposit-services-to-payment-services-use ratio was higher than average, as the cost of payment services did not unduly reduce deposit revenues. Oslo Banken's strategy might be paraphrased into a sales argument for an unbundling invasion of banking:

> Buy your priced high-return deposit services from us rather than from the established banks, for we give you a better deal. Buy other cost-generating services from the established banks, who provide them free.

Innovators not only make sure that they set the rules of the game according to which other actors entering the customer's business constellation must play by innovating on offering architecture, they also rewrite the existing rules of the game. For successful offering redefiners, those who are reconfigurers, the new rules of the game manifested in their offering innovations become those which redefine the roles of other actors. Consider the burgeoning field of automated manufacturing in which a battle now rages. The combatants are the companies making automatic manufacturing devices, such as robots, and those such as EDS and large accounting firms, who have established specialized departments for consulting and systems integration in the field. At the time of writing, the latter appear to have the upper hand.

In most fields, there tends to be a logical sequence by which customers make their purchasing and co-production decisions. Early positioning at an operational interface such as factory management levels by manufacturers gives way to a more financial or strategic interface by the suppliers of advice or systems integration, which come to dominate the customer relationship. Together with the customer, they outline the 'rules of the game', according to which the equipment manufacturers must then play.

Reconfiguration strategies also succeed when they provide quicker responses than competitors can; particularly if these concern speeding up feedback on fast-changing customer value creation The success of the Italian fashion house, Benetton, is in our view strongly related to their superior way of integrating point of sale (market) information on offering performance to the organization of production. Their central computer in Treviso, near Venice, is connected to points of sale and feeds back market-trend information to production. In this way, Benetton matches produced types and colours with evolving client fashion-making more efficiently than most competitors. This speed allows them not only to spot trend changes earlier but also to reinforce them selectively, making them not only fashion followers but, through effective matching, fashion-makers.

Note that the reconfigurer role that Benetton has created for itself is reflected both in terms of internal operations such as those outlined above as well as externally. Here Benetton's matching configures actions, roles and relations among the myriad subcontractors they employ.

Swatch did something similar. It adapted product innovations from the 'flattest watch' design developed by SMH, the company which owns the Swatch make, which it had first manifested in the premium 'Concorde Delirium' watch. This design basically halved the number of components required, as the casing was made to hold much of the movements. Swatch adapted the design and decided to produce as much of it in plastic as possible, obtaining unprecedented reliability, cost and scope economies in watch production. This made it possible for the offering to be made in relatively small series, with short lead times, and with great product redesign potential. Halving the number of components had a quadratic effect on reliability, which made it possible to replace the exceptional faulty units instead of repairing them, given the extraordinarily low unit costs. This in turn made it possible to make the Swatch available through non-specialist distribution systems, which meant that the productive knowledge of distributors not specialized in watches but who supplied fashion and personality enhancement could be shared at very low, marginal, cost. In short, Swatch reconfigured the roles of metal-working and precision-movements guild producers traditionally associated with the industry in Switzerland, watch repairers, jeweller's shops traditionally distributing watches, alternative retail outlets, and indeed customers—who could use a timepiece as a fashion accessory for the first time. The average Italian Swatch owner has as many as six Swatches.

The Swatch offering is based on the idea that a watch can be a lifestyle-enhancement tool, much like a Benetton sweatshirt. A Swatch is cheap, and is not expected to have a very long life span. It is available in many places, where it can be bought more or less on impulse by customers. The highly technical breakthroughs were found to be capable of fitting the whims that make up significant value creation for a relevant part of its customer base. But they are also fitting other more rational consumers, who want good value for money, with values which include a particular sense of aesthetics, a particular way of fitting in socially, and a particular self-image; to which Swatch has learned to contribute most effectively.

22 The need for continuous improvement: reconfiguring as a process

Concept research

The renewal of configurations, the process of reconfiguring, is necessary to a firm's survival in a changing environment. Quantum-leap innovations assigning new roles to actors come from *continuous* watching, from 'concept research' (Van des Heijden, 1993) activities enabling the firm to identify and seize opportunities, to respond to changes. Many such changes are detectable in customer value-creation logics, as well as in the value-creation logics of any other counterpart—be it a supplier, a regulator, or whatever. When successful, they are not only reflected in the new co-productive formulae of the offering, they also reset the rules of the game for whole constellations of economic actors. Reconfiguring is hard work, for it implies introducing new interfaces and reshaping old ones, redesigning value-creation systems, reallocating roles, recentering trust-building and trust-testing mechanisms, and so on.

Van der Heijden's idea of 'concept research' implies the conceptual suspending, 'bracketing' or ignoring of established organizational boundaries. He suggests that managers assume that all counterparts are in a singular organization, and that they have that type of freedom to reallocate activities, roles and relations. Be this as it may, the new configuration will consider boundaries not only as functional elements articulating role and specific activity *distinction* but also, and more importantly, as functional elements which permit the joining of actors playing their newly assigned roles and carrying out their respective activities. Much of the required success is on how well the integration such boundaries entail is ensured. Thus special attention will be given by strategists in the future to transaction costs and to the role of integrative infrastructures, be they physical like optical cables or inter-personal such as cultural compatibility and understanding.

Companies capable of focusing their attention on ever more effective integration internally and with the outside world are likely to be more successful than those exclusively focused on internal improvements. Continuous improvement in reconfigura-tion as a process means enhancing the *meta-competence* of effective integration of productive resources, including constantly reas-sessing both the firm's and the customer's knowledge/competen-cies. Thus, effective reconfigurers will be effective 'conversation holders', catalysing an effective dialogue between competence development and customer development.

Treating knowledge as an asset

The offering, as we saw, transfers knowledge to customers via human 'here and now' activities and via pre-packaged 'goods'. While it is evident that humans producing 'here and now' value are knowledgeable, it is less obvious that the pre-packaged goods are the result of the past actions of knowledgeable people, be they inside or outside the company.

The knowledge transferred via here-and-now human activities is a direct function of human behaviour. They are typically en-abled by the pre-packaged knowledge in the supporting products and systems. As we saw in previous chapters, value for the customer as well as for others in the value-creating system can be defined in terms of the 'density' of options effectively made available. But here the density is understood not only as a function of action options but also in terms of the amount of knowledge brought to bear upon actors in specific time/space units.

The effectiveness of persons in a knowledge-creation system depends on the team they are involved with; the tools and the network they have access to; the form of management structure and other corporate support systems they are a part of; the human resources and professional development programmes that they have participated in; the information, 'theory', 'world-view', values, ethics, codes of conduct that guide them. It is only when individuals act that they have any impact on value creation—but note that thinking while sitting on a park bench also implies action!

Action does not necessarily follow from being knowledgeable, educated, experienced or even motivated. When these and other resources are mobilized into action we can speak of the existence of 'competence'. Knowledge as such may be dormant in an organization, and may therefore not represent competence. Competence is measured in terms of effectiveness of action, and thus represents an asset in the organization which must be fostered and developed. Also, competence is subject to how much knowledge can be put at the disposal of actors, so as to enhance their effectiveness.

Thus companies build their reconfiguration skills on two assets: (1) customer bases (relations with customers which give one a role supporting customer value creation) and (2) competence enhancement. The reconfiguring *meta-competence* ensures that assets (1) and (2) develop each other as much as possible. The developments of this metacompetence are manifested in offering redesign, which is where the matching between asset (1) and asset (2) becomes palpable, tangible and... testable. In the next, and final, part of this book we review how this has been successfully done by four economic actors in different industries and countries.

PART THREE

Illustrative Cases

Introduction

In this third and final part, we provide four examples of businesses which have been or are being reconfigured. These examples illustrate how the observations and theoretical descriptions in the preceding two parts of the book are manifested in everyday, practical terms. The four examples are:

- *IKEA*, which has become the largest retailer of home furnishings in the world;
- *Ryder System*, which has over the years been a key reconfigurer of the truck transportation business in North America;
- The 300 independent *Danish pharmacists* and their *National Association*, which have played a key role in the reconfiguration of health care in that country; and
- The *Compagnie Générale des Eaux* and the *Suez Lyonnaise des Eaux* group, which have played an important role in rendering French local authorities more effective public-service suppliers through reconfiguration.[1]

The outline of this third part of the book is depicted schematically in Figure E.1. As is evident, the cases are made to illustrate three key aspects of business reconfiguration covered in this book:

- The *what*, which includes *who* and *with whom*;
- The *how*, including insights on *when* and *for how long*; and
- The *why*, which implies a *what for*.

---

[1] An earlier publication on the IKEA, Danish pharmacists, and Générale des Eaux and Lyonnaise des Eaux Dumez cases is found in Normann and Ramirez (1993a).

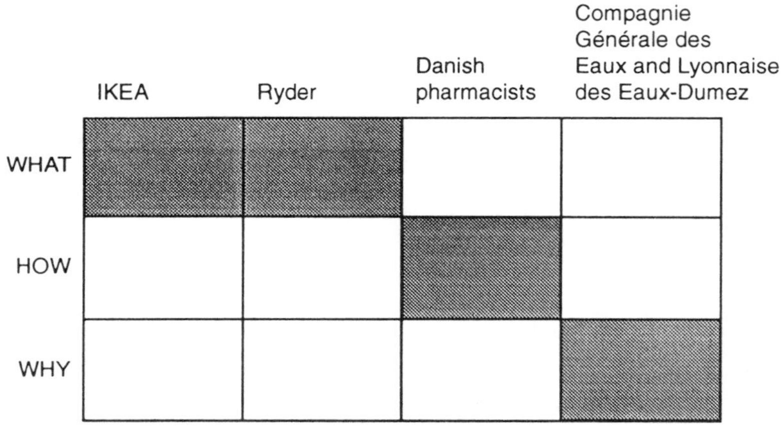

Figure E.1 The 'what', 'how' and 'why' emphasis of Examples 1–4

Example 1: IKEA and the 'what'

In only 40 years IKEA has become the largest furniture retailer in the world. With 142 stores and 5.860 billion US$ worth of turnover, IKEA is present in 1997 in 29 countries. Upon opening the 1993 French issue of the IKEA catalogue, you quickly come to a page where you find the following script (our italics):

We develop our own products (to keep expenses low)	*You* help yourselves (touch and try the products yourselves)
We are the kings of flat packages (less transport and warehousing costs and easier for you to handle)	*You* take away your purchases yourselves
We buy in large quantities (and command lower prices)	*You* assemble the products yourselves (tools and instructions are included with all packages)

This 'co-productive' script is unique in the sense that it is *explicit*; but all offerings imply such scripts. The 'script' which an offering consists of allocates activities, and thus roles, to economic actors. These roles imply a commercial relationship which co-produces value.

We do not buy a haircut, however 'passive' we may be in the barber's while the barber cuts our hair, without thinking of our own activity logic as well as the barber's: which barber's location, speed, availability, style, best fits with our own set of activities (meetings, interviews, press conferences, dates, parking ease)?

As we shall see, one of IKEA's strengths has been to understand where it fits in its own customers' value-creation universe, and in turn to fit itself in an intelligent way into its suppliers' and partners' value-creation system. This is evident from IKEA's beginnings, when as a teenager its founder ran an operation delivering fish, grain and newspapers by bicycle to locals in a small rural Swedish community. Ingvar Kamprad, IKEA's founder and still today the main owner, personifies the thrifty and dynamic business philosophy of his native Småland, a region in the south of Sweden.

IKEA has become something of an exemplar of this philosophy, and its very name summarizes this. IKEA stands for *I*ngvar *K*amprad, the entrepreneur; *E*lmtaryd, Ingvar Kamprad's home farm; and *A*gunnaryd, his home village. The fact that Småland lost 50% of its inhabitants to Denmark and the United States in the mid-nineteenth century due to migration caused by extreme poverty has much affected IKEA's business philosophy. It is in such hardship that one can find the roots of hard-headedness, initiative, enterprise, modesty, parsimoniousness and dynamism which characterize both the region and the company.

Kamprad incorporated his operation in 1943, when he was 17. Demonstrating the gift he had for appreciating how new possibilities changed the potential ways in which his customers could act to create value for themselves, in 1947 he added mail-order capabilities and the then revolutionary ballpoint pen. This enabled his customers to shop from home, and to order (as well as write other things!) with greater ease. Kamprad edited his first catalogue in 1950, including some furniture items for the first time.

Just as Kamprad had demonstrated his having a 'gift' for seeing opportunities in changing his customer's value creation, so too was he gifted in spotting underutilized capabilities elsewhere, which could make him more efficient if he convinced others to utilize them better. The accommodations he demanded others to make in this sense in effect implied reconfiguring the activities and roles of these 'others', who became partners. He also constantly innovated to reconfigure his own and his customer's activities. Thus, upon creating his first catalogue, Kamprad also made a deal to use the spare capacity in the local milk-delivery trucks, thereby supplementing his catalogue-based cost-effective customer access. When the dairy stopped this service, Kamprad moved into the local town, Almhult, where he opened his first

Example 1 109

showroom in 1953, and found alternative delivery systems, some of which were based on self-service at his shop.

A further step in making the overall system of co-production more effective by changing activities and roles, and thus relationships, implied what, with hindsight, was a critical breakthrough in 1956. Kamprad and his colleagues started shipping the furniture unassembled, in parts, to customers, to facilitate transportation. This entailed a 'division of work' formula between IKEA and its customers which is still critical to the firm's success: IKEA will *design* the furniture, *find* suppliers to manufacture its components and *package* the furniture into flat packages; the customers will choose it and assemble it themselves.

The gains that flat packaging allows IKEA to make in terms of cheaper transportation and warehousing, whose costing is in cubic metres which are thereby saved by greater 'density', are shared with the customers. The customers pay even less than the transport/storage savings this implies by also assembling the furniture themselves, thereby avoiding IKEA's steep labour, assembly and associated administrative costs.

By 1957 IKEA had a turnover of 17 million Swedish Crowns (about US$3 million at that time) and in 1958 opened its first shop, pioneering much of the self-service work-sharing concept which it outlines in its French catalogue, as seen earlier. According to Goran Carstedt, now president of IKEA North America, the shop was overrun with customers early after its opening, and someone (Kamprad himself, perhaps) had the idea of letting the customers into the back-shop warehouse to serve themselves. Reconfiguration here is seen as a process of responding to everyday problems and *then* reflecting on how the practical solution could be built into the overall value-creation system to prevent that problem recurring. This is what Argyris and Schön (1978) have referred to as double-loop learning. Double-loop learning is a necessary element in an effective reconfiguring process.

Understanding that novel work-sharing works if the risk-sharing is perceived to be advantageous, in 1963 IKEA reached an agreement with the Swedish standards agency to label the furniture as having passed certain quality standards, manifested in the very visible '*Möbelfakta*' label. The reputation for 'quality' that people associate with Sweden, perhaps only equalled by the view they have of German quality, contributed further to enhance the acceptability of Kamprad's reconfigured activity sets.

The acceptability of reconfiguration which insufficient attention to managing different types of risk assumes is patent in the fact that IKEA's first internationalization was determined not by marketing but because of a boycott by several local furniture producers. They were threatened by IKEA, and in effect forced Kamprad to look outside the country for suppliers. Kamprad's capacity to spot possibilities outside the industry, shown earlier with milk deliveries, was extended here: now windowmakers produce table tops for IKEA, shirt-makers produce cushions.

IKEA's first non-Swedish shop opened in Norway; the first non-Scandinavian one in Switzerland. Today, the Nordic countries only account for 29% of the total turnover, East Central Europe 15%, and the rest of Europe account for 33%; while Asia and North America account respectively for 18% and 4%. In 1997, IKEA totalizes 36,400 co-workers of which only 5,500 are in Sweden. 31,000 are in Europe, 4,100 in North America and 1,000 in the Rest of the World.

IKEA sites its shops with a so-called 'potato field philosophy', which consists of finding cheap land outside major urban areas. Given IKEA's characteristic intelligence for fitting its customers' logics in innovative ways, usually the 'potato field' has a convenient motorway access near it, although sometimes there is not much else near the store when it opens. The approach accepts that it takes about three years for potential IKEA customers in that market to become accustomed to the reconfiguration of roles that it proposes; that is the time it takes for IKEA's new shops to achieve what it considers to be 'mature' sales levels. With several new shops opening yearly (22 stores were opened over the last 3 years) this delay is not insignificant. To speed up this 'maturing' process, IKEA has developed 'co-production' formulae with customers which are meant to extend and 'deepen' the relationship over time, as is, for example, the case with creating a 'club' concept for families.

IKEA offers its Family Club members discounted holidays, discounted access to leisure facilities in the area where the shop is located, discounted subscriptions to magazines, and even insurance, which is produced in a joint venture with a Swiss insurance company and distributed by IKEA. Club members have their own stores in the IKEA shops with discounted travel equipment,

Example 1 111

periodic mailings on special offers and discounted meals at the
IKEA restaurants.

These reconfiguration ideas, integrated as an overall business
approach, yield impressive results. In the UK for instance, IKEA
managed to achieve 2.7 times more sales per square foot than the
industry average in 1993. In the French furniture market, which
decreased by 4.7% in 1991–2, IKEA managed a 5% increase in
turnover.

The idea of co-producing with the customer, getting the customer to gain from assembling furniture kits, thereby saving on
labour, storage and transportation costs, is only one aspect of
IKEA's success. At least as significant is the extraordinary reconfiguration it managed to carry out with suppliers. Dealing directly
with manufacturers, cutting out middlemen, and engaging many
of these as long-term partners is a core part of IKEA's success. It
is no accident that when Ingvar Kamprad retired from the position
of CEO in 1986 he was determined to keep an eye on the 'buying'
function as well as the 'design' process.

Of its approximately 1800 suppliers in over 65 countries, IKEA
directly controls (e.g. through equity) only between 5% and 10%,
and does not intend to integrate further. About 50 of these 1800
suppliers are the 'hard core' upon which it relies. To do so they
have in effect become not only 'suppliers' but also partners and
customers. IKEA will often provide them with services enabling
them to supply IKEA with what it requires.

IKEA's decisions as to which suppliers to relate with rest partly
on quality-to-cost ratios (the 'minimum' necessary elements for
effective co-production); partly on IKEA's local buying philosophy, which allows it to become more easily accepted in a given
market (a long-term version of 'co-producing' acceptability);
partly on the opportunity which such relationships present to
learn about local business conditions (a long-term version of
'co-producing' the business's futures); and partly on minimizing
transport costs. The fact that some 500 of its 1800 suppliers are in
Eastern Europe, for instance, much facilitated IKEA's early en-
trance there.

Overall, one can observe a trend to deconcentrate supplies from
its original sourcing, all in being loyal to its trusted established
sources. One of these is the Swedish institution which trains and
employs handicapped workers, which has supplied up to 10% of

what IKEA sells world-wide. Today, approximately 30% by value of what IKEA acquires is produced in Scandinavia, although Scandinavia now only accounts for only 20% of the turnover. Today the major part of the purchases (82%) are still made in Europe (9% of the total IKEA purchases are made in Sweden, 25% in Germany, and 48% in the rest of Europe).

'Supplying' co-producers are sought and evaluated by IKEA 'buying offices' around the world, which pre-select suppliers for a centralized decision-making process situated in Almhult. Keeping good relations with proven suppliers and finding new trustworthy ones is a key to success, particularly if one considers that IKEA's sales have grown eightfold in the last ten years. Being out of stock needs to be avoided at all costs to maintain the reliability image that is so central to the firm's reputation (which amounts to proper risk-sharing in the offering's co-productive nature) and growth.

The co-production which IKEA manages with selected suppliers are 'win-win' formulae that render explicit, and thus manageable, aspects which often remain implicit and undermanaged with competitors. IKEA's co-productive philosophy is thus present in what in 'value chain' concepts would be considered 'upstream' as well as 'downstream'—with 'suppliers' as well as with 'customers'.

The buying function is linked to a sophisticated proprietary logistical system that is essential to IKEA's reconfiguration success. In Europe, where IKEA has 73 shops, it has ten warehouses in which it integrates the components produced by different suppliers into kits for assembly by customers. It is in the warehouses that much of the actual integration of activities to ensure effective matching with the activities outsiders (suppliers as well as customers) takes place. In effect, 10% of what is received in these warehouses is sent on directly, after appropriate 'bundling' (or configuration), in kits (supporting self-service by customers), to IKEA shops. For it is part of IKEA's co-productive success that different components of a given piece of furniture often come from different suppliers; for instance, the back of a chair being made in the Czech Republic, its feet in France, and the screws joining both made in Spain.

While roughly a third of each shop's surface is warehousing space (double Habitat's average ratio), IKEA needs the ten warehouses to store and integrate the large-volume orders it places

Example 1 *113*

with its suppliers. This 'storage' cost may appear to be contrary to the direct-buying, just-in-time philosophy in vogue today, but the production constraints of the manufacturers/suppliers of IKEA components require large production runs to obtain low unit costs. These translate into large-volume commands which offset the considerable storage costs, still significantly reducing unit costs. The fact that 90% of what IKEA's shops offer across the market is identical helps to secure the advantages of such scale economics. While these economics give IKEA substantial cost advantages, with enhanced co-productive quality, they could be improved: today only some 10% of its suppliers deliver directly. For the others IKEA still requires external transportation support.

If IKEA were to become more amenable to following fashion, like Benetton or Swatch, it would have to develop a different co-productive logic from the one it has pursued so far. It would have to reorient its logistical and warehousing systems significantly to take into account how its customers' becoming older, richer and more bourgeois reflects their tastes. The fact that this is happening because of demographics and per capita income increases in its Western country markets, albeit more slowly than teenage fashion changes for Swatch, and inasmuch as logistics are a central piece of IKEA these developments pose a challenge to the organization. Logically, although we ignore the link, they offer an explanation for the acquisition of Habitat by Kamprad.

Another aspect of IKEA's co-productive infrastructure is the way information collected from cash registers in IKEA shops around the world is sent for centralized analysis to Almhult, the operational, but not official, group headquarters. In a way that reminds us of Benetton's infrastructure, these analyses orient automated orders from the nearest warehouses to the shop. The nearer the warehouse, the less the cost of supplying the shop, and thus IKEA's investing in warehousing today precedes shop openings. For instance, a massive warehouse unit, near Lyon in southern France, was opened in 1993 prior to attacking the Spanish market and further developing its Italian foothold. This mega-warehouse, which began operating with a capacity of 66 000 square metres was expected to reach 110 000 square metres. It was expected to free capacity in Switzerland, Austria and Germany previously used for the French and southern European markets, redeploying it to secure support for its aggressive growth in

Eastern Europe, including eastern Germany. Yet these warehouses will continue to serve the French and Italian/Spanish markets, as no one warehouse carries 100% of what is sold in IKEA's shops. To give an idea of the size of such warehouses, one should consider that IKEA's largest, in Almhult, with 135 000 square metres, holds enough items to fully furnish 30 000 three-bedroom apartments...

With rail, air, and motorway access enabling easy and efficient co-productive access, the Lyon facility will allow IKEA to move 1000 cubic metres per day (the equivalent of twenty to thirty truckloads). Each shop receives, on average, about 10 truckloads of material a day. One part of the warehouse stocks items which have faster turn-around times, another stocks large orders from single suppliers for longer periods. The shop/warehouse (internal co-production) relations are integrated by a proprietary IKEA computer system called 'Terminal' which is centred on a DEC Vax minicomputer using an Oracle relational database. IBM 3090 computers connect this system to outsiders; internally it integrates over 400 printers, 44 terminals, and ten PCs to deal with customs and administrative matters. It says a lot about how important co-productive 'boundary-bridging' is considered to be in IKEA that none of its warehouses has a 'computing department'. The care for the co-production-enabling system is with the users, and only one person is a full-time technical resource for these.

Given that IKEA is still private, profitability figures are not publicly available. Yet Anders Moberg, its president since 1986, has stated that IKEA International re-invests 15% of its turnover; and various independent observers calculate its profitability at 8–10%. In any case, it is clear that the profitability is sufficient, for IKEA's growth has not required access to stock market financing.

IKEA understands the value-creation logics of its customers during the purchase experience, in the pre-purchase, and in the post-purchase periods. The IKEA catalogue, which is printed at over 45 million copies per year in ten languages, is in Sweden the third most widely available book after the Bible and the telephone directory. Fifty per cent of IKEA's marketing budget is spent producing the catalogue and the other half promoting it. It is available free of charge at IKEA stores and is mailed to IKEA Family Club members. A considerable proportion of IKEA's approximately 11 400 active products are portrayed, including year-long prices

Example 1   115

(again, a form of effective risk-management in the co-production it offers). Virtually all store visitors, 100 million in 1996, take one and then lend theirs to friends, neighbours and family.

The IKEA shop architecture funnels visitors to the second floor, where products are displayed, before customers re-descend to the first floor, where they pick up items they have chosen upstairs to take home. Both the catalogue and the showrooms offer co-ordinated room sets which place items for sale in the context of everyday living. The leitmotif for the co-ordination is Swedish design, providing functional, stylish furniture that gives the rooms in question a feeling of lightness and space. 'We try to give people as many ideas as possible, which gives them the confidence to give an idea a try' says IKEA. In one of its brochures, they say *'We've nothing against cutting down on costs—but we'll never do it on ideas'*. Manifesting in its own way the concept of 'leverage value' we have presented, IKEA states that 'wealth is to [be able to] realize your ideas'. Clearly, many of its employees are believers, believing that the company they work for allows 'everyday people' to become wealthier in this sense, having good furniture at competitive prices in their homes.

For the shopping stage of the co-production, IKEA also offers spacious free parking for all its shops, which in other countries are painted in the bright yellow and blue colours of Sweden. Perhaps no other retailer in the world uses its national origins so intensely in its brand and image marketing as does IKEA. One way to understand this is that it considers the 'Swedishness' it brings to its side of co-production an important element for its targeted co-producing customers. The shop entrances have amenities such as supervised childcare/playground facilities, strollers for children, wheelchairs for the handicapped, and a receptionist desk; all designed to facilitate co-production with different customer segments. Cafés and restaurants serving Swedish food as well as local/international cuisine are also located on the second floor, all with IKEA furniture. A Swedish food outlet is situated after the cash checkouts for the main shopping, together with a fast-food/stand-up bar outlet serving Swedish hot-dogs.

The shops are designed around key shopping 'moments of truth' (Normann, 1978, 1991). The displayed furniture and furnishing items carry simple readable labels that indicate the name of the product (which often sounds very Swedish and is almost unpronounceable, including vowels such as 'ø' and 'ä'), the price, the colours in which it is available, the materials of which it is made, its dimensions, how to take care of it/clean it, and the place in the shop when it can be ordered or picked up. All enhance the customer's own activities in co-producing effective shopping and/or maintenance activities. There are virtually no sales staff; the staff are there to enable the self-service shopping processes. For instance, they take orders for bulky items which will be prepared by warehousing personnel for pick-up downstairs. The clients do most of the work themselves: they choose, compare, in many cases order and pick up without the 'help' of pushy salespersons.

After payment, customers place their compactly packaged acquisitions in distinctive trolleys provided by IKEA and then put them in their cars. If they cannot manage to fit their purchases in their cars, IKEA will lend them roof racks or sell them at cost. If necessary, they will contract with a transportation company for home delivery, also virtually at cost.

Once the customer has arrived home with all acquired compact packages, the next step is unpacking and assembling the parts into actual pieces of furniture. IKEA provides all required tools and assembly instructions.

IKEA's compact packaging increases the density of what it offers per space and time unit, which is a way of increasing the 'value' it enables suppliers and customers to co-produce. Density implies less waste, and more options per actor in time and space; more wealth per action, if one will. This is evident in ratios such as sales per square foot, transport and storage costs per square metre, choice per visit, etc. IKEA states in its brochures that 'every one of our...home furnishing products is designed to allow the individual customer as much freedom of choice as possible', that is, to increase the options for living space arrangements for a given individual as much as possible per space/time unit and per dollar: 'The catalogue makes it possible for customers to decide what to buy in the peace and quiet of their own homes. And it helps them to plan their finances too' says one of their brochures. The translation of this setting of 'peace and quiet' to the actual shop is designed to *'take the hassle out of shopping'*, making the second experience in the IKEA shop resemble the first at one's home as much as possible. IKEA in this respect considers itself to be in the 'family outings' business.

Example 1 117

The concept of 'quality' that IKEA has developed fits this density notion of value like a glove. Ingvar Kamprad—as opposed to many CEOs today—explicitly warns that 'quality should never become an end in itself'; instead, quality 'should be adapted to the consumer's needs'.

IKEA's way of transforming furniture retailing has been called a 'category killer' by retail analysts, which is the trade view of what we are more generally calling 'reconfiguring'. Other so-called retail 'category killers' are Toys 'R' Us, Walmart and PC World. Typically 'category killers' 'kill' a set of competitors in a given market by offering volumes of discount goods. But IKEA in our eyes stands apart from the others. In having redefined the design/procurement process, making itself the centre of what in effect is a circle absorbing different offerings, repackaging them and astutely positioning them in the right place in the absorption circles of its customer, IKEA has managed to develop a living form of the type of business logics which we see as the emerging winning logics in almost all kinds of business situations.

The flexibility that IKEA has built into the constellation of co-productive arrangements reduces the usefulness of traditional role definitions such as 'supplier' and 'customer'. By re-establishing the density of home furnishing offerings, IKEA has succeeded in squeezing more profitability out of physical and human resources than almost anyone else in its industry. IKEA could in traditional terms be considered a 'hollow' corporation, having 'outsourced' most of its manufacturing. Yet such a view would miss the strategic insight that makes it work. IKEA does not simply add value, it enhances the value creation of its 'suppliers' and its 'customers', influencing the very nature of such value.

Example 2: Ryder System and the reconfiguration of the truck-leasing industry[1]

Ryder System highlights the growth potential of a company which matches the value-creation logics of its core customers with its evolving competencies as the guideline to reconfigure its industry. The company understood the importance of breaking out of the limitations of the value chain concept. In the early 90s, Ryder Systems dominated the industry in many ways, as it had understood that its business was much more leasing trucks to customers who do not want to have their own.

Ryder System's business, as we will see in detail below, is to work with customers to help them to organize and manage their transportation and business needs, not only in terms of equipment, but also including drivers, insurance, logistics, etc. As a result of Ryder System's persistent search to find new ways to help its customers, the company has taken on new roles that extend beyond the leasing activity which gave Ryder System its origins. The rearrangement of roles between actors it has achieved in its industry is a good example of what we call reconfiguration.

From a one-man truck-leasing company started by 21-year-old James Ryder in 1934 in Florida, Ryder System in 1997 is a company with 42 000 employees and 1996 revenues worth US$ 5.5 billion. In the early 90s, it was operating the world's largest full-service truck-leasing and short-term rental company; North America's largest new automobile transport company; the world's largest independent jet-aircraft engine maintenance

---

[1] Much of this chapter is based on extensive research by our colleague Ralph O. Walton III. This case concerns a time period closed in 1994.

Example 2   *119*

and overhaul company; a leading aircraft-leasing and parts-distribution company; and was a leading provider of mass transit and school bus services throughout the United States. Ryder System was the market leader in most of its operating areas.

A key to Ryder System's success in the early 90s is that despite its many subsidiaries, it has concentrated on only two business areas — after having disposed a wide range of diversified interest acquired in the 1970s. In 1993, Ryder System was only active in what they termed Highway Transporation Systems and Aviation Services, but within these two business areas, Ryder System was providing a very wide range of services to, and with, its customers[2]. It has, for example, a logistics division to help truck leasers to manage their warehousing and loading capabilities, as it can achieve scale economics for most of its customers which they cannot obtain on their own. The relative sizes of both business areas as well as the divisions making them up are shown in Figure (E.2.).

Ryder System's business areas in 1993 were the result of a carefully constructed expansion based on matching its competencies with the

---

[2] In 1998, Ryder System is only active in what they term Integrated Logistics and Transport Solutions. It means that they disposed of the Aviation services activity.

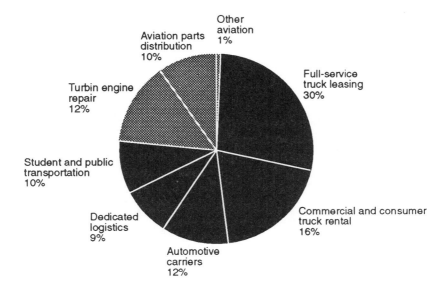

Figure E.2.   The Business composition of Ryder System

evolving requirements of its customers. The company's expansion, in our terms, is based on the search not only for *additional customer bases* (for example, the leasing of buses for school district authorities) for its current competencies but also for better ways to 'leverage' the value of the Ryder System offering to its current customers. It is a search, in other words, for *additional competencies* for its current customer bases.

Figure E.3 shows four stages in Ryder System's evolution from a simple truck-leasing company to a fully fledged, competence-customer base integrating company in the 'transportation services' business. Ryder System's evolution has not been as linear as Figure E.3 may indicate. A glance at the history of the company shows that it has made mistakes in how it developed in the past, particularly in terms of diversifying in ways which led to building *away from* existing competencies rather than *on* them. But Ryder System appears to have learned from such mistakes in the 'double-loop' sense referred to above and become a better reconfigurer as a result. To get a good view of how this happened, we briefly review this history.

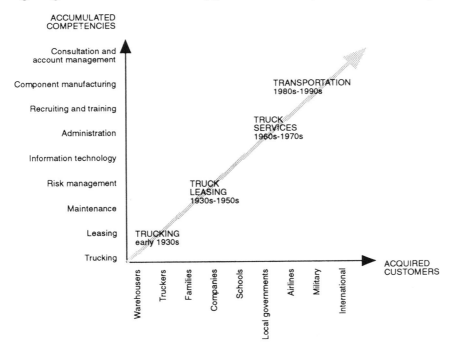

Figure E.3   Ryder Systems reconfigurated evolution

Example 2   121

1930s to 1960s: birth, success and the first diversification

Ryder System was the first truck-leasing company in the United States, and its debut coincided with, and benefited from, the massive construction and improvement of highways in the 1930s. Building its strength on this vast network of better highways, highway trucking began to rival rail as a means of overland haulage. World War II further increased demand for trucking, stretching the existing transportation system to capacity, and Ryder System's trucking and leasing operations grew accordingly.

In 1952, Ryder System made its first foray away from 'pure' truck *leasing* into *trucking per se* with its US$2 million acquisition of the Great Southern Trucking Company. Founded in 1933 by L. A. Raulerson, Great Southern had grown into the South-east's largest freight carrier, with some routes as long as 1100 miles. With this acquisition, Ryder System's revenues were quadrupled, and it became a very large freight carrier as well as a major truck-leasing concern.

Ryder System, Inc. was created in 1955 to absorb Ryder Truck Rental and Great Southern, and the new company offered shares to the public. Shortly thereafter Ryder System bought more than 25 companies in 5 years. The larger companies included Baker Truck Rental, Inc. of Denver, Colorado; Barrett Truck Leasing Co. of Detroit; TSC. Motor Freight Lines, Inc.; the truck-leasing business of Columbia Terminals Co.; Dixie Drive-It-Yourself System, of Alabama; the truck-leasing business of Barrett Garages, Inc. of San Francisco; Morrison International Corporation; and International Railway Car Leasing Corporation.

This impressive acquisition drive cannot be considered 'diversification', as most of the acquisitions were truck-leasing companies. However, the significant growth in size was a 'mistake' in the sense that the company failed to install sufficient financial controls. This forced Ryder System to write off US$2 million in bad debts by 1960, and profits consequently dipped from US$2.7 million in 1959 to about US$1 million in 1960. A central accounting system was implemented to remedy the problems, and steady growth returned in the early 1960s.

In 1965 Ryder System sold its freight carrier division (of which Great Southern Trucking Company was the anchor) to International Utilities (IU), a diversified holding company. The trucking division grew under IU's direction, which had kept the Ryder name, until its spin-off in 1982. The Ryder System company focused on the fast-growing truck-leasing business, and despite common misconceptions, since 1965 it has not operated as a freight carrier.

The sale of Ryder System's trucking services represented a return for the company to its original core business of truck leasing. At this point, Ryder System was again involved in only one specific business area, albeit through a conglomeration of companies in the same industry.

In our view, strategic expansion of a company's resources should be based on the acquisition of *competencies* to be offered to existing customer bases, rather than the acquisition of competencies unrelated to these existing customers. With the additional competencies, a company takes on additional, new responsibilities for and with its customer base, and expands to offer these to new customers as well. It thus rearranges the established separation of work, roles and relationships in the business, thereby reconfiguring it. The complementary way of expanding is to build on existing competencies and apply them to new customer bases. As we shall see, Ryder System developed both ways, at different times.

In this perspective, the divestment of the trucking function was an effective first step to reconfiguration. However, as we will see below, James Ryder, the strong-willed founder and original president of the company, expanded his company indiscriminately over the decade following the sale of Great Southern, catching in his net companies that fit our reconfiguration approach to growth (e.g. insurance companies) as well as those that do not fit it, (i.e. technical schools). These are the companies that imply diversification away from, rather than supporting, existing competence-customer matching. Reconfiguration through the effective matching of customers and competencies would finally occur later in Ryder System, once the misdirected diversification acquisitions were discarded.

1960s to 1970s: uncontrolled diversification

The late 1960s saw the appearance of new services in truck leasing and rental in the US market. In 1967 Ryder System began offering

Example 2   123

a one-way truck-rental service. This service had been invented and popularized by the U-Haul Company several years earlier. Ryder System started with 1000 trucks and expanded the one-way fleet to 7630 in the first year. Competition in this field grew rapidly; Hertz Corporation and E-Z Haul, a division of National Car Rental System, Inc., entered the business. As a result, the one-way market became oversupplied, and Ryder System's one-way unit, which was intent on capturing the market, got off to a slower start than it had expected. In 1968 it offered to buy U-Haul International Co., but the deal did not work out. Ryder System expanded its one-way dealership network through an agreement with Budget Rent-A-Car. While many competitors dropped out in the early 1970s, Ryder System did not, selling surplus vehicles when necessary, and in 1987 finally managed to surpass U-Haul's one-way rental, albeit briefly.

In 1968 Ryder System decided that its competencies could serve a new customer base, and it entered the new-auto carriage business by acquiring M. & G. Convoy, Inc. In January 1970, Ryder System's expertise in automotive carriage services was recognized as superior and they were hired by General Motors and Chrysler for the transport of new cars to dealerships. At this time, and for similar reasons, Ryder System also entered the dedicated contract carriage business, where it provides customized transportation and distribution services for new clients.

In the late 1960s Ryder System misread the importance of growing from established competencies to new customer bases or from established customer relations to new competencies, and made the mistake of trying to enter new competencies *and* new customer relations simultaneously. It thus diversified into services unrelated to transport leasing or to its customers. In late 1969 it made a foray into the growing temporary-help industry, initially placing office and industrial personnel, later technical help. In 1969 and 1970, it also acquired several trade schools, offering courses in car mechanics, truck driving, and a number of other technical fields. In 1970 Ryder System purchased Mobile World Inc., a distributor of mobile homes and a mobile-home-park operator and franchiser.

Ryder System also made acquisitions that were related to existing customer bases or competencies. For example, it acquired an insurance firm, Southern Underwriters, Inc., and formed a joint venture, Ry-Air Inc., to provide pick-up and delivery services for 27 airlines in New York.

While Ryder System's main business—full-service truck leasing—remained strong in the early 1970s, the company's management was spread ever more 'thinly' over its growing number of new businesses. In 1973 the oil crisis enticed Ryder System to purchase Toro Petroleum Corporation of Louisiana to ensure a steady fuel supply for its trucks, but the acquisition proved a somewhat rash move. The value of Toro's oil reserves dropped as oil prices fell a few months after the purchase. Ryder System had bought high and ended with a US$7 million loss.

Other problems related to the diversifications caused a 13 cent per share adjustment in the company's 1973 audit. These adjustments reflected calculation differences in receivables from the education unit, tax assessments on the mobile-home subsidiary, and reserve assessments on the insurance subsidiary. Ryder, in effect, made the mistake of considering its *meta-competence* of integrating customer and competence development as 'separable from' the two latter. One becomes a good *meta*-integrator by knowing one's customers and/or comptences well; one cannot abstract away from these. This is the lesson that Ryder Systems learnt, at a cost.

Because funds were channelled away to pay for misguided diversification costs, the truck-leasing and rental businesses had to borrow to finance an expanding fleet. Ryder System's debts grew to more the US$400 million, four times shareholders' equity. This led to Moody's Investors Service downgrading Ryder System's rating on commercial paper in late 1974. Ryder System lost US$20 million, and the company's investors became deeply concerned; the board of directors began to question James Ryder's abilities.

The 1973-4 recession took a heavy toll on the US automotive industry, and thus on Ryder System's vast contract carriage and automotive carriage operations. Although the company's core business of truck leasing and rental did reasonably well despite the hard times, company borrowing came to be seen by displeased stockholders as having become out of control. They were unhappy with the company's troublesome diversification acquisitions of the late 1960s and early 1970s, and demanded a refocusing of attention on Ryder System's original 'core' businesses.

Example 2 125

In 1975 James Ryder, under pressure from the boardroom and his bankers, announced that he was seeking a 'more professional manager' to run the still-growing company. In the summer of 1975, after disposing of unprofitable 'diversified' subsidiaries like Toro Petroleum, Miller Trailers, and most of the technical schools, James Ryder stepped down as head of the company that he had founded 41 years earlier.

Ryder's failure was his attempt to create a conglomerate without a business idea based on the coherent dialogue between competence and customer development. As we will see below, the truck rental, automobile carriage and dedicated contract carriage activities share and add to competencies related to Ryder System's basic business of leasing trucks and transportation management. The temporary help, trade school, mobile homes and oil industries require competencies that are almost totally unrelated to the truck-leasing business, although James Ryder's aggressive acquisitions did bring in some companies that his successors would use as building blocks in the reconfiguration of their industry. The achievement of these successors in weeding out unrelated business areas transformed Ryder System from an unwieldy conglomerate into an ideal example of a company that builds on matching its competencies and its customer's logic, often advantageously, adapting to industry developments (i.e. deregulation). As such, Ryder System has redesigned the activity sharing between customers, suppliers, and the company on an ongoing basis ever since.

The 1980s: turning the company around

James Ryder's successor was Leslie O. Barnes, former head of Allegheny Airlines. Barnes, then 59, inherited a somewhat tattered company. He quickly pared the debt-to-equity ratio from four-to-one to three-to-one, and he sold Ryder Liftlease Inc., a small but troublesome subsidiary, as well as the remainder of the technical schools.

Refocused on its primary businesses, Ryder System bounced back. In the late 1970s the company grew internally and through acquisitions in the full-service truck-leasing business (to which we will return below)—leading an expanding market. According to Barnes' calculations, only 38% of the US private truck fleets were wholly owned by 1980, down from 60% in 1970, as the great majority of the fleets were now at least partially leased. This trend was a wave which Ryder System 'surfed' better than most.

Following the election of Ronald Reagan as president of the United States in 1980, deregulation became the key industry trend. In 1983 new rules concerning single-source leasing allowed private fleet operators (manufacturers, retailers or food companies that haul their own raw materials or finished products) to get—for the first time—drivers through Ryder System as a part of the leasing agreement. Ryder System set up a special dedicated contract carriage division to respond to the new demand for custom leasing. By the end of the decade, Ryder System provided not only leased trucks but also drivers. It supplied management system design to specialty freight companies like Emery Air Freight, retailers like Montgomery Ward, Sears, and J.C. Penney, and newspaper publishers like Dow Jones and the Miami Herald.

Deregulation also allowed private shippers to solicit outside freight business, effectively allowing direct competition with independent truckers. Ryder System, who always understood its customers' business and how it could best position its competencies to support them well, immediately responded to this new opportunity and bought three new freight packaging companies to book return loads for private shippers leasing from Ryder System. This allowed it again to take advantage of the economies of scale it enjoys in relation to its customers, and to make these customers benefit from this advantage.

In 1986 a major federal tax law revision made it even more attractive for private fleet operators to lease their fleets rather than buy than it had been in the past. As Ryder System had been continuously expanding its truck fleet (between 1984 and 1988 it nearly doubled its size) it was well positioned to take advantage of this new demand. More and more fleet operators turned over the hassles of fleet purchase, maintenance and insurance to Ryder System, allowing them to concentrate on the production and sale of their products. From a customer relationship based on *enabling* clients to do what they did better, Ryder System thus reconfigured to a relationship where it *relieved* them of many activities that were

Example 2 127

outsourced to Ryder System, freeing clients to concentrate on their own business.

We have maintained that a key to successful companies lies first in an accurate assessment of a customer's value-creation logics. Successful companies then determine how they can help their customers with their own business concerns. This entails reassessing how products and services enable their customers to create value for their own customers as well as redesigning these to best match the customer's value creation. The redesign of the roles each actor takes by reallocating activities and thus changing relationships is what we term reconfiguration. Ryder System exemplifies this well.

The highway transportation services area is Ryder System's traditional business, accounting in 1992 for 77% of the company's revenues. Ryder System's offering in this business area includes the vehicles and virtually all the support services a customer needs for its operations. As opposed to typical truck makers, whose language and mind-set has been traditionally on product-centred issues such as torque, horsepower, on-board electronics or chrome, Ryder System's concerns have been derived from those of its customers: turn-around times, operating costs, fleet yields, downtime, etc. Ryder System has attempted to respond to the customer's value creation so that the customer in turn can best fulfil its obligations to its own customer: manufacturing companies, retailers, parents, car makers and distributors, etc.

The full-lease offering shown in Figure E.4, for example, is designed to cover all the problems related to fleet ownership: upfront investment, space and utility costs, administrative time, maintenance facilities and qualified technical expertise, reliability of older equipment, fuel or load efficiency of older equipment, fuel storage, compliance with environmental regulations, or re-couping resale value. With the full-service lease, the former fleet owner transfers all these concerns to Ryder System—a basic example of the reallocation of activities that leads to reconfiguration.

Ryder System has reconfigured the industry so that the relationship of a customer to its truck leasing firm is broader and richer than the simple rental of a truck. It has taken over activities that were previously carried out by customers or by third parties and by other suppliers. Ryder System's highly successful Dedicated

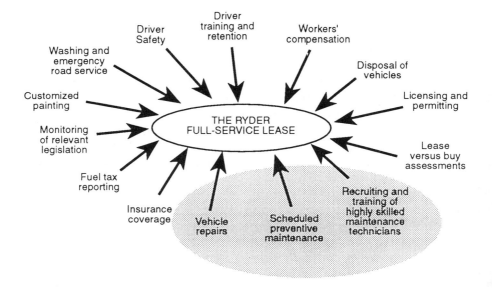

Figure E.4   Ryder full-lease

Logistics division, for example, is devoted entirely to tasks previously taken care of by the customer. These activities include:

- Lead logistics programmes
- Dedicated contract carriage
- Warehousing
- Cross-docking
- Subassembly
- Inbound delivery of components
- Outbound delivery of finished products.

Ryder System's contract with General Motors' Saturn plant is an example of the extent to which tasks can be reallocated, that is, to which the industry can be reconfigured. Ryder System's Commercial Truck Rental division rents trucks to GM to bring components to the plant. The rental of trucks, however, is just one small facet of the offering. GM utilizes Ryder System's dedicated contract carriage product which enables their Saturn plant to achieve just-in-time delivery of components when and where they are needed anywhere in the production system. Ryder System manages

Example 2 129

GM's inventory for inbound materials, even warehousing its own facilities parts and materials for the GM plant. The company is performing what has traditionally been done internally by its customers for them, freeing GM to do what *it* does best.

The plant's inbound logistics is handled by the Dedicated Logistics Division which rents vehicles from Ryder System's Commercial Truck Rental Division. The Automotive Carriage Division handles the oubound logistics to the dealer's door. Ryder System not only acts as Saturn's transportation department, but actually helped them to design the plant in terms of maximizing in-/outbound logistics.

Expanding on current customer bases and competencies

Beginning in the late 1970s, Ryder System, encouraged by the basic business's performance, once again began to seek acquisitions. But Barnes, unlike James Ryder, was inclined to test new ventures on a small scale before fully committing to them; and chose these in areas more closely related to competencies and customer bases than had been the case earlier. In 1978 a parcel-delivery service, Jack Rabbit Express, was acquired. A small property and casualty reinsurance company, Federal Assurance Co., was added to existing insurance operations, for reconfiguration implied new risk allocations, and Ryder System's business's success rests partly on the effective assuming, management and distribution of risk.

In the early 1980s, new tax laws encouraged growth into new areas. Ryder System began shopping for a financial services company in order to take full advantage of available tax credits. Insurance and financial services were the obvious choices because of Ryder System's existing insurance competency and of the importance of risk management in reconfiguration as well as of financial information in leasing. After futile efforts in 1982 to acquire a majority of Frank B. Hall and Co., the third largest insurer in the United States, Ryder System expanded their financial services activity in 1983 by becoming 80% owners of a pension fund specialist, Forstmann, Leff, Kimberly. In 1985, the company acquired the Municipal Issuers Service Corporation. By 1988, Ryder System had amassed an insurance operation consisting of writing policies, doing claims work, auditing, safety work, underwriting and pricing. Arguably, the formation of Ryder System's Insurance Management Services division was driven more by the desire to offer more comprehensive services to leasing customers than by capitalizing on acquired competencies. This is evident in the fact that Ryder System sold its insurance business in 1989. Presumably its capacity as a wholesale buyer offset the need to keep these competencies in-house.

The company at this time also built on its automotive carriage activities: in 1977 it acquired a major car carrier, Jamesville Auto Transport Company, for US$10 million in common stock. Its automotive carriage operations were by then profitable as a result of the industry's rebound and its implementing tighter financial controls. During the 1979 downturn in the automotive markets, Ryder System's automotive contract carriage unit, representing 16% of the company's turnover, still made a profit. In the 1980s, Ryder System acquired two new strategically located car carriage firms to help to improve efficiency through its capacity to reduce the number of trailers sent back empty.

In 1985 Ryder System entered the school-bus leasing business, acquiring a new customer group for its established competencies, and quickly grew to be the second-largest private student-transport company in the United States. It also entered public transportation system consulting and leasing in the mid-1980s.

In the early 1980s Ryder System entered another expanding transportation field in which established competencies could be of help to a new customer base—aviation leasing. In 1983 it acquired Aviation Sales Co. Inc. and its subsidiary, General Hydraulics Corporation, of Florida, an aircraft-leasing and spare-parts firm. In 1985 Ryder System bought Aviall, Inc., a turbine-engine repair and overhaul firm located in Dallas. Aviall was also an aircraft parts distributor. Several other smaller leasing and repair companies were acquired. By late 1986 aviation services comprised about one-fifth of Ryder System's revenues, and in 1987 the division branched out overseas with the purchase of Caledonian Airmotive Ltd in Scotland. This Scottish subsidiary serviced the big engines on British Caledonian Airways' DC-10s and 747s, among others. Caledonian Airmotive complemented

Example 2 131

Aviall's operation both geographically and in services offered. By 1988, just six years after entering the aviation services business, Ryder System was the world's largest jet-engine overhaul and rebuilding company, the largest aviation parts distributor, and one of the largest aircraft and jet-engine leasing companies. Ryder System's aviation division counted 300 commercial airlines among its clients, and dozens of private operators. By 1988 revenues from aviation approached US$1 billion.

In 1991, Ryder System elected to leave the airline leasing market due to the risk in the underlying business. The 1980s were a time of heady expansion, of billion-dollar orders, of rapid addition of international routes and of mergers. When airlines' passenger volume was threatened, Ryder System merely lowered prices and continued to order new or leased aircraft. But in the past 3 years, at least six major US air carriers have either closed down or gone into bankruptcy. International Air Transport Association (IATA) figures show that the cumulative losses of US$11.5 billion world airlines made on their scheduled international services in the three years to the end of 1992 were greater than all the net profits since such services began 74 years ago (*The Economist*, 30 October, 1993). Ryder System's deep understanding of the risks and financial logics of the business allowed it to see, earlier than most, that aircraft leasing was an opportunistic venture whose time had gone.

In total, Ryder System spent US$1.1 billion on 65 acquisitions between 1983 and 1987. However, unlike the acquisitions in the 1970s, these were intended to build on what the company saw as its two core competencies: asset management, especially maintenance, and distribution logistics. Thus the aviation activities (for the most part related to maintenance of equipment) and the school bus activities (efficient student ride logistics) were logical new customer bases for Ryder System. The expansion through the acquisition of new customer bases was accompanied during this time by expanding its competencies, increasing activities and services made available to its customers.

Example 3: Danish pharmacists and their national association

The emerging logic of value creation, and the dialogue between competencies and customers it creates, presents every company with a stark choice : either reconfigure the business system to take advantage of these trends, or be reconfigured by more dynamic competitors. To exploit these trends, managers must reconsider the business potential of their chief assets: the company's knowledge base, its customer base, and how the two relate to each other, basically through their offerings. In doing this, they often must reposition or re-invent the company's offerings to create a better fit between the company's competencies and the value-creating activities of its customers. As a result, they need to create new business arrangements and, sometimes, new social and political alliances to make these offerings feasible and efficient.

Just over ten years ago, Denmark, like many other European countries, began to reform and deregulate its state-funded health-care system in an effort to address rising costs. Denmark's network of some 300 privately owned pharmacies is made up of privately owned firms that are heavily regulated. For centuries, they held a legal monopoly on the sale of both over-the-counter and prescription drugs and have also had the right to manufacture generic ones. They have thus competed with their suppliers on everything except patented pharmaceuticals.

The Danish state sets pharmaceutical prices in a negotiation that looks at margins on drugs in the context of overall pharmacy profits. Until recently, this negotiation was annual, which meant that if pharmacy profits suddenly rose, then the state would cut drug prices the following year to bring profits back into line and

Example 3   133

share this 'windfall' with the taxpayers. In practice, pharmacy profits never rose or fell very much because, while the system guaranteed a high degree of security, it did nothing at all to encourage efficiency, innovation or gains in productivity.

Decades of this system also left the pharmacies highly vulnerable to competition if they ever lost their monopoly. Also, the need to control health-care costs had prompted several stakeholders to call for the complete nationalization of the pharmacies, so as to make regulation complete.

Therefore when the political system began to focus on health care, the pharmacies and their professional organization, the Danish Pharmaceutical Association, thought that they saw the writing on the wall—an altered industry, new competitors, new dangers—and decided to take a hard look at their assets to see if they could find new opportunities as well. They concluded that their network of local pharmacies had two potential but still underutilized strengths.

The first was the corps of local pharmacists themselves, who were well-educated health-care professionals. In Denmark, as elsewhere in the West, most critical decisions about patient health care were made by other actors in the system: primarily the doctors who wrote prescriptions and the pharmaceutical companies that developed new drugs; not by the pharmacists, who had been 'outconfigured' by the medical doctors and the pharmaceutical companies over time.

The second strength was the fact that the network of 300 pharmacies and 1600 subsidiary outlets throughout the country was exactly this: a *network*. This represented a highly effective access channel to the Danish population. It was found that people respected and trusted their local pharmacists, and as the general public became better informed, people began to see that good health was not something they could delegate to the government or the health-care industry. Health depended on personal behaviour and individual lifestyle choices. The public was hungry for information and advice on how to live a healthier life.

These two strengths gave the pharmacists an opportunity to reposition their offerings, and thus reconfigure their business. Beyond being where prescription drugs and other pharmaceutical products could be bought, pharmacies could also comprise a comprehensive source of health-care information and services. More of the offering could be manifested in the pharmacist and interactions, and the relative importance of goods and transactions would be commensurately decreased.

This first role reconfiguration led the Association to adopt three interconnected goals :

(1) To develop pharmacies into a more advanced knowledge and service business, building on established but heretofore underutilized competencies;
(2) To establish a solid, productive relationship with government health-care agencies, developing a new 'value constellation architecture' (the creation of value through multiple relationships); and
(3) To reorganize the Association along lines that would help to achieve goals 1 and 2, changing the roles and relationships of its units.

In addition to these articulated aims, the Association had several tacit goals. It would do everything possible to preserve its monopoly in pharmaceuticals retailing, as well as its strong position in wholesaling. It would lower operating costs by increasing pharmacy productivity. If it achieved this, it also would support the enacting of legislation giving pharmacies incentives to work more efficiently.

As seen above, strict state regulation had meant that efficiency had had a low priority for Danish pharmacies, all in having allowed for a modest profit. There had thus not been any reason for pharmacies to streamline operations. The possibility of deregulation changed this. The Association and its members would need to compete more effectively on every front, all in seeking a new legal environment that would render the improvement of efficiency and the expanding of services beneficial to all. This took place in 1984, when the Danish parliament passed a new law whereby the state would set prices for two years at a time; if pharmacies could generate higher margins than predicted, they could keep the difference, at least until the next negotiation. Immediately, the pharmacies began to rationalize operations and cut staff. Net profit rose significantly with periodic setbacks as the Ministry of Health lowered prices.

Example 3   135

At about the same time, the Association took two other steps to strengthen its position as a reconfigurer in the emerging reconfiguration. First, in an effort to divert attacks on its monopoly in drugs retailing, the Association tried to downplay its direct competition with the pharmaceuticals industry by setting an 'independent' subsidiary to carry out its drug manufacturing. Second, it managed to emerge from a series of mergers in pharmaceuticals wholesaling with a 25% controlling interest in a wholesaling giant that had 70% of the market.

The pharmacists simultaneously continued the reconfiguration of their retailing by broadening their traditional role, delivery of conventional pharmaceutical 'hardware' (in other words, selling drug goods), into a concept they called Pharmaceutical Care, which would emphasize the 'software' (service, information, advice) aspect of health-care delivery. They saw Pharmaceutical Care as a way of creating and legitimizing a strong reconfiguring position within the changing health-care system by securing access to the core of their customers' value-creating activities in health maintenance.

Beginning in 1982, and continuing into the 1990s, the pharmacies and their national association devised and carried out a series of strategies that sought to involve private customers and health-care institutions in new relationships by innovating on offerings. They expanded the range of goods sold to include health and diet foods, high-quality herbal medicines, skin-care and other related items. To enhance responsiveness and increase their effectiveness as middlemen transforming this role to that of logistical integrators of the reconfiguring constellation in which they were embedded, they installed a computer prescription service and an electronic pharmaceuticals ordering system. Like IKEA, and considering the risk-management allocation that is so vital (literally) in their business, they worked with suppliers to develop new quality-control measures and informational labelling.

To render their customers more effective health-value creators, they upgraded their customer-information services, installed computers to access health information, and published and distributed self-help books and preventive health-care pamphlets. An interesting example of this strategy to help customers to become more effective at being healthier was that they initiated their own anti-tobacco campaign, selling literature and anti-smoking chewing gum, and, as of 1986, offered stop-smoking courses that combined education and group therapy. In understanding the opportunities that their customers' changing value-creation activity logics afforded, they developed home health-care packages for newly discharged hospital patients, self-care packages for routine health problems such as measuring blood pressure, support packages for health-care institutions and associations, and preventive-care packages for customers with special nutritional or dietary needs.

These strategies met with limited success, at least in the beginning. In fact, the pharmacies had set themselves a difficult reconfiguring task, which in a sense amounted to having their cake and eating it too. They were trying to protect their monopoly in pharmaceuticals retailing; to improve their position in wholesaling; to take on a more central role in drug training, education, and quality control; and to greatly enlarge their activities in health counselling, preventive medicine, and the sale of herbals, health food and diet products. The other actors in the health-care industry tended to see the last reconfiguration efforts in particular as encroachments on their own heretofore exclusive preserves. This reconfiguration effort, which could be interpreted as predatory expansionism, was not helped by the pharmacists' making larger net profits than ever.

The Association, as a reconfigurer, saw all this in quite a different light, of course. After decades of strategic hibernation, the pharmacists were rising to the business and social challenges of fundamental health-care reform in ways that served different types of citizens better. Indeed, given their history, they arguably showed themselves surprisingly ready and able to modernize their operations, update their expertise, redefine their customer base, rethink their business, and tailor a fresh fit between competencies and customers, both new and old. But, as was discovered, neither the state and its administration nor the customers themselves (let alone counterparts with established vested interests and political 'weight') were able to cope with so much sudden change. The state moved so slowly in deregulating and reforming Danish health care (84% of health care is still in the public sector) that the Association's innovations kept running into regulatory barriers and political pitfalls. Also, the different parties that the Association had thought it could mobilize around a common

Example 3   137

reconfiguration based on its new concept of wholistic, preventive health maintenance—doctors, hospitals, long-term care facilities, even patients—tended to greet proposed innovations with suspicion and resistance, almost regardless of the circumstances.

The anti-smoking campaign, for example, amounted to a test of the doctors' response to the idea of pharmacies operating in a counselling role, as pharmacists had done long ago—before doctors had reconfigured them out of this role. To the Association's disappointment, although to no-one's great surprise, the doctors viewed the programme as an incursion on their own professional territory. They applied pressure and forced the courses off the market. Similarly, the pharmacists found little demand for their home health-care packages for newly discharged patients, partly because hospitals and the public health insurance agency viewed them as competitors and declined to recommend the service. Self-care packages also fared poorly. True, on Blood Pressure Day in 1991, thousands of Danes visited pharmacies all over the country for blood pressure and cholesterol readings, but, as a general rule, people wanted their doctors to continue to make even simple tests and recommend even basic treatments free of charge, as they had always done in the past.

Clearly, the pharmacies were doing something wrong, and it was not hard to see what it was. The new strategy itself was a good one as far as it went—re-invention of a centuries-old business to fit new social and commercial realities, development of denser offerings, more interaction with suppliers and customers to co-produce value. The problem was credibility—a form of risk management implicitly built into roles over time, almost imperceptibly. Denmark's individual pharmacies had always been private businesses, and their professional Association had always been a non-profit organization. But with this reconfiguration effort, the Association had strayed further into outright commercial competition. With customers, pharmacists enjoyed a hard-earned reputation for professionalism and excellence that was very robust and could weather much reconfiguration. Within its industry, the Association's reconfigurer role was earning it a reputation for sharp elbows.

If the Association was going to succeed in this role it urgently needed to improve its relations with the political system and other stake-holders in the health-care sector. To achieve this end, it had to behave a little less like a competitor (win–lose changes) and think more seriously and consistently about the (win–win) co-productive constellations in which it wished to operate. It needed to rethink its concept of reconfiguration process and principles, and push its new strategy further accordingly.

The Association is a purely voluntary organization of independent pharmacists. It has long had the authority to negotiate drug prices with the government, but it had never had the power to force its strategic thinking on individual member pharmacies. Yet the process of business reconfiguration implies building new competencies. The government may have moved slowly in learning to understand their new roles in the health-care complex, but the pharmacies had also moved slowly in learning the skills, the behaviours, the competencies that investing their new roles entailed.

In 1969, the Association had established an educational centre outside Copenhagen to centralize the training of licensed pharmacy technicians and to offer its pharmacist members continuing, post-graduate education in new pharmaceutical developments. In the 1980s, as the Association's new reconfigurer role began to take hold, the school broadened its programme to include courses in marketing, service management, customer orientation, and business skills. Now the old educational facility also had its own role reconfigured, and it became a tool for promoting ideas and disseminating the Association's new understanding of its business, roles and relationships.

As successful co-production at the reconfiguration level cannot afford too much win–lose competition, in 1990 the Association sold its drug-manufacturing subsidiary and withdrew from pharmaceuticals production for the first time in its history, eliminating once and for all its direct competition with the pharmaceutical companies.

Internal reconfiguration of the Association meant that in 1991 it divided its activities into two distinct 'poles'. It assembled its for-profit business assets—computer operations, wholesaling and the profits from the sale of its drug-production subsidiary—into a separate company that operated according to normal business principles. Strategic planning (i.e. where 'reconfiguration' is determined) and the co-ordination of educational, informational and social services remained not-for-profit activities and stayed

Example 3   139

in the hands of the Association itself, strongly backed by profits from business activities.

In its external reconfiguration attempts, the Association successfully increased its efforts to build alliances with Denmark's national organization for the elderly and disabled, as well as other national associations for those with heart disease, epilepsy, asthma and diabetes, among others. It now also works closely with the Danish Consumer Council in areas such as drug information and labelling, which over time build the goodwill and trust upon which reputation, that great asset for the risk-allocation element required by effective reconfiguration, rests.

The Association's efforts in the redesign of the national health-care sector won it international acclaim, and this exposure helped it to forge alliances with sister organizations across Europe and around the world, which proved most helpful in supporting its reconfigurer role at home. In 1985 the Association urged the World Health Organization (WHO) to work more closely with pharmacists, and this led to the establishment of the Europharm Forum, linking pharmaceutical organizations in WHO's European region. In 1988 WHO issued guidelines recommending that pharmacists assume a central role in health-care systems as drugs advisors *par excellence* to patients, doctors and other professionals.

The Association even took part, in 1993, in an international, multi-centre study of the pharmacist's role in drug therapies. In Denmark, the research project was working with 300 asthma patients in a study of pharmacist-assisted asthma therapies. Because the study incorporates a new division of responsibility among patient, doctor and pharmacist, the Association appointed two doctors—a professor of medicine and a clinical pharmacologist—to the project's steering committee. This is an instance of reconfiguration where 'strong elbows' perceptions are no longer a blockage, as 'win–win' solutions seem to have been found.

The result of these efforts has been striking. In 1992 the Association re-introduced its anti-smoking courses in a joint venture with Europharm Forum and the WHO. This time, due to the Association's alliances and its international standing as a credible reconfigurer, Danish doctors found themselves with *de facto* recognition of the pharmacies' counselling activities. The programme was a success, and the WHO wants to export it to other parts of Europe: the Association's reconfiguring has thus become international.

Also in 1992, the Association's business subsidiary acquired 10% of Denmark's only ambulance operator, creating a co-productive alliance between two businesses with the same set of customers. Among other things, this alliance has revived the home-care concept with a system for dependable delivery of drug, support and security services to the elderly and to patients recently discharged from hospital. But because it represents an access channel to customer's value creation that is accepted by these as 'normal' (patients do go back to their homes by ambulance), the reconfiguration that it implies was not subjected to the reaction caused by the 'suddenness' associated with earlier efforts.

Overall, greater operational efficiency has allowed individual pharmacies to increase their net profits steadily while reducing gross profits substantially, a strong argument for preserving their retail monopoly. Moreover, the Association, while one of the world's smallest, was economically one of the world's strongest in 1993, with more than US$200 million in assets, not, of course, counting the value of the independent pharmacies themselves. In 1992 the Association developed a plan that takes reconfiguration and co-production into the twenty-first century with new initiatives that saved Danish taxpayers more than US$16 million in the first year.

The pharmacies' reconfiguration struggles are no doubt far from over. Their business environment is also a political one, a fact that has complicated their efforts to work with other health-care players to produce new offerings and enlarge the opportunities for value creation available to the average citizen–customer. Yet what the pharmacies discovered was that reconfiguration could be devised to make both political and business sense.

The re-invention of any business constellation is at least partly a matter of thinking through the social implications of change. In the end, new offerings linking them to many counterparts (associations, doctors, international bodies, patients, other suppliers) have gradually allowed the pharmacies to obtain a far higher return on their knowledge base and their customer base than they ever enjoyed in the past.

Example 4: The Compagnie Générale des Eaux and the Suez Lyonnaise des Eaux group: the 'why'[1]

In many Western countries, public infrastructure is a wholly public responsibility. The city (or state, county, or regional authority) governments put out tenders for public-works projects to be built according to designs and specifications supplied by the city and its consultants, and is paid for by having the city issue bonds and assume debt. Construction is carried out by outside suppliers under contract with the city; operation and maintenance of the completed system is done by the city or contracted out, often piecemeal and for brief periods. The advisers controlling this project are on the city's payroll or work for it as consultants. This has been the most standard in the Anglo-Saxon world, and is evident in most of Europe as well.

As opposed to what happened in many other countries, a distinction between the *provision* of public services (which remained a public responsibility) and their *production* (which was contracted out to private operators) was made in France in the nineteenth century. This practice of 'delegation' gave rise to a number of private company 'concessionaires'. They built the required infrastructure and operated it to obtain a return on

---

[1] The original example was written in 1993. Major changes have occurred since then. In June 1997, Lyonnaise des Eaux-Dumez and Suez (previously the group's main shareholder) merged, becoming "Suez Lyonnaise des Eaux".

Compagnie Générale des Eaux has a new Chairman since June 1996, when J-M Messier replaced G Dejouany. In March 1998, the Générale acquired Havas Communication.

The example was updated in March 1998.

investment. This applied to rail services, canals, gas and water, and later to electricity distribution, airlines, roads and other 'public' services.

Some of these French companies have evolved into corporations that have no real counterpart in other Western countries. Today two major players dominate this business: the Groupe Générale des Eaux and the Suez Lyonnaise des Eaux Group. In 1997, they had a turnover of US$28 billion and US$32.5 billion, respectively. And, in 1996 (i.e. before the merger of Lyonnaise and Suez) they had revenues of US$317 million and US$225 million respectively. Between them, they provide drinking water to 40 million French residents (25M from CGE and 15M from Suez-Lyonnaise). They are the two major players in water supply worldwide: Générale provides nearly 65 million people in water distribution and/or purifying, while Lyonnaise is the largest private water company in the world, with more than 70 million consumers in five continents. Yet to think of either as a water company fails entirely to capture their business, their business logic or how the strategic game is being redefined.

In addition to water, both Générale and Lyonnaise provide cities and towns with everything from heating systems, sewers and hazardous waste treatment to construction, old building management, street cleaning vehicles, and TV or Telecommunication networks. In Toulouse, for instance, Générale not only manages the city's water distribution but has also developed the Aqualand recreation centre and is an investor in the city's cable TV network. Suez Lyonnaise des Eaux manages several cities historical monuments, art museum, or public gardens as the 'Jacquemart André' museum in Paris or the 'Baux de Provence'. Suez Lyonnaise des Eaux owns 16 cable networks and, as such, is the first cable operating company in France.

As we stated in the *Harvard Business Review* (Normann and Ramírez, 1993a) these many activities could be seen—from a value chain point of view—as a rather uncontrolled form of diversification. But from the point of view of the framework we present in this book it is not 'diversification'. Instead, it is a very good example of how holding a 'conversation' between customer value-adding activities, on the one hand, and the evolution of core competencies, on the other, structures business development as such.

Example 4   143

The Compagnie Générale des Eaux was founded in 1853 as a water-supply company serving French municipalities. It has always been a privately owned company. It started to provide new services to its customers immediately after World War II, as the municipalities started to demand investment and developments for these in the light of post-war reconstruction, particularly in urban heating and energy control. The Lyonnaise des Eaux has similar origins. It was created in 1880 by the Crédit Lyonnais bank to supply cities with water. Note that this was not unique at the time; during this same period the Chase Manhattan bank also had a strong presence in water distribution. The Lyonnaise grew through acquisitions, of a canal in Cannes for example, and grew into domains such as the distribution of gas and electricity. With the nationalization of these sectors after World War II, it lost much of its gained ground and had to start again from a narrower base. Compared with the Groupe Générale des Eaux, which, as shown below, has arguably pursued the type of strategy described in this book on a fairly consistent basis since the war, the Lyonnaise des Eaux Group first responded to the nationalization by diversifying. In a way which evokes Ryder System's history, it developed its multi-service reconfigurer approach only after divesting many of the diversified activities and returning to the core activity of water and related services. In 1997, CGE (217 000 people the largest private employer in France) is still substantially larger than Suez-Lyonnaise des Eaux (180 000 people). Yet, it is an explicit objective for the latter to become the first worldwide supplier of 'services collectifs de proximité' in the 5 coming years.

Using the delegation of public services as their starting point, the French water concessionaires, and particularly Générale and Lyonnaise, have reconfigured roles and relationships into a different business logic. The core business of these companies was in the recent past depicted in French as 'aménageurs de villes'. The French word 'aménager' means, at the same time, to develop, to plan, to work out or lay out, to fit out, to convert or adjust, to make or build. This type of 'fitted-out town design and planning', because of difficult economic conditions, needed to be financed by concessions, where the cash generated from the use of the infrastructure after it has been built will pay for its design and construction—and thus the 'aménageur' also becomes a concession operator. As we shall see at the end, more recently the 'aménageur de villes' role was reoriented to a 'service collectif de proximité' one, in effect positioning the customer's customers as a key target.

The concession reconfiguration means that it is not taxpayers who pay for all the public infrastructure made available to them: the concession usually implies that users pay more than non-users. In the concession system, what is elsewhere short-term relations between private suppliers and public clients is extended over time—in some cases for 30 or 40 years. This means that the concessionaire:

- Designs the project and its specification (instead of having the city and its consultants do so, saving public expense).
- Raises the capital (avoiding the taxpayer paying for municipal debt through local taxes).
- Builds the infrastructure (which means that it also acts as a construction company).
- Manages the assets (preventing city administrations from becoming overly bloated with public employees).
- Bears the risks (an essential part of offering design and redesign hedged by length of concession).
- Pockets the operating profits (which is the price the city pays for the reconfiguration, and for being relieved of carrying all the risk).
- Assuming a large part of the local government's authority and responsibility in order to do so (in some cases having the right to enter private premises, and even to expropriate property on behalf of the city!).

However, the concessionaire must also do all it can to ensure that its concession is renewed, for such lengthy contracts are worth very large sums. This 'turbocharges' the *'conversation'* between competency evolution and customer logics, as the opportunity costs involved are considerable. Thus as an executive in one of these companies explained to us in 1992: 'Our commercial people do not have the right to say 'no' to a client request; if one of the companies in our group cannot produce what the client requests, we will create a company to satisfy this need.'

Example 4   145

Because of industry consolidation, and because of the success of the two main contenders in this game, concession renewals were, in a recent past hardly ever lost to competition. This, combined with a threat on the concession system in France (both companies feared in the early 90s that the concession system would not last forever in light of changing contexts), drove both companies to internationalize. This strategy has so far proven to be most successful. In 1997, 15.6% of the Générale turnover in the Water activity is made abroad, 27.9% in the Energy sector, and 37.6% in the Construction sector. The Suez Lyonnaise, leader in the international water market, is offering services to 70 million people in the world of which 14 million are in France and 56 million outside France.

The dual push to internationalize, and to maintain an evolution of core competencies to match developing customer activity developments, have made Générale and Suez Lyonnaise develop skills that their non-French competitors seem to lack. In a sense these skills are reconfiguration *meta-skills*, that is, skills relating to the design of the organization rather than to the production of goods and services. The French companies have consistently increased the sophistication of their inter-organizational design necessary for the success of the wide-ranging reconfiguration they have masterminded. One can argue that their expertise is precisely that of developing, acquiring, integrating, matching a broad cross-section of technologies and knowledge, and focusing them on their customers' continuously evolving value-creation logics. Thus, in 1997, Générale has some 2500 subsidiaries and Suez Lyonnaise has approximately 2000 subsidiaries, ranging from very small (one person!) to very large companies. These are grouped according to specialization or *métier*. Both groups are global, with very autonomous subsidiaries—who often will create new jointly owned subsidiaries to address an identified customer opportunity that no single subsidiary can match on its own. Synergy is obtained by regrouping *métiers* at as many levels as feasible, as is the case, for instance, with 60 different identified *métiers* at Générale. A typical resulting value constellation is shown in Figure E.5.

Beyond the internal integration of diversified skills in which both companies have come to excel (a key *meta-competence* in its own right, as we have seen), both groups have pursued a

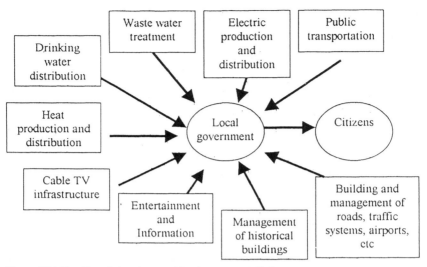

Figure E.5 The French 'aménageur' business constellation

complementary tactic, building partnerships and alliances with outsiders with strong local presence or competencies where the companies are relatively weak. These alliances permit the concessionaires to bring in denser offerings to existing customers and to enlarge their customer bases, both without having to incur the 'normal' required expenses to do so. Générale has, for instance, formed special alliances with European companies such as Rhône Poulenc that, as one executive put it, are 'clients as well as suppliers to us'. Générale des Eaux also made an agreement with Compagnie de Navigation Mixte to explore how to collaborate in the provision of public transportation; with Veba it created a common subsidiary to develop the East German water treatment and distribution market, and through OTV, a 100% owned subsidiary, it acquired 45% of the 'green' Danish company Krüger. In March 1997, Générale initiated exclusive and unexpected negotiations with the French State Railways SNCF in order to develop an alternative long-distance telecommunication network for the whole of France. In 1998, it acquired Havas Communication.

In the same way, after it merged with Dumez in 1990, Lyonnaise discarded a number of Dumez's previous diversification to finance the creation of joint ventures with counterparts which can better help it to co-evolve competencies and customers. It

Example 4 147

sold GIM, which makes individual homes, as well as 10% of the fifth largest German construction company, Dywidag. It sold also its 24% holding of Groupelec, its holdings in UK water authorities Wessex and Severn Trent, and United Westburn, the Canadian electrical distributor making up the bulk of the electrical materials distribution business. The financial resources that these disposals raised were used to meet the financial costs which the Lyonnaise-Dumez merger generated, as well as to develop the *meta-competency*. This involved the purchase of 26% of the Compagnie Parisienne de Chauffage Urbain from EDF, the state electricity monopoly, obtaining an extra 25% of the total Parisian market for urban heating; and the purchasing of SDEI, the last remaining independent water distributor in France.

The results are manifold for both companies; a good example is the collection of refuse and street cleaning and the waste fuel co-generation plants, enabling 10% of the residents of Paris to be heated with steam produced through incineration. The integrated solutions which their meta-competency enables them to bring to the customer is proving a strong competitive advantage *vis-à-vis* competitors who are more limited in scope, such as Bechtel in engineering, Veba in energy systems or Browning-Ferris Industries in waste management.

In terms of competency development, it is not surprising that both companies are advanced R&D innovators in the fields in which they are most competitive, a result of effectively matching competency and customer developments. In the small French town of Méry-sur-Oise, Générale established the first commercial chlorine-free municipal water-treatment system in the world; the 800 Suez Lyonnaise researchers organized along a decentralized international network of research laboratories (France, Great Britain, and Asia) earned 40 new patents in 1997 and were awarded the 'innovation champion' prize in France.

With such advanced knowledge, the companies have been able to cater for customers in the private sector as well as in the public one. With this added advantage of running the competency/customer base matching effectively, allowing the balance to expand in ever-larger circles to include broader sets of customers, the companies have become leaders in emerging markets for 'green' industrial services, such as waste management. This market was estimated at US$34.5 billion in 1991 in

Europe alone, and is expected to double by 2000. A Générale subsidiary runs Europe's largest hazardous-waste-treatment facility in Limay, outside Paris. The Suez Lyonnaise, via its subsidiary Sita, dedicated to waste management, signed in 1997 with the American group Browning-Ferris Industries (2nd actor worldwide in the waste management market) an acquisition agreement concerning all the non-US activities of BFI. This allows SITA to become the first European operator for waste collecting and management, and the third major player worldwide.

Tailor-made public service package development, supported by leading-edge competency, is not only a source of profit growth but is also a powerful force in dealing with competitors to complete deals successfully as new opportunities emerge. The cities of Buenos Aires and Macao exemplify how the business idea of these companies works in practice. In Macao, for instance, a first contract was awarded to Lyonnaise des Eaux for water distribution and waste-water treatment. Subsequently, the Lyonnaise des Eaux acquired Macao's electricity production and distribution company. This led to building a new electricity power-generating station in this Portuguese colony, and to developing the largest water-analysis laboratory in Asia. This experience is helping Suez-Lyonnaise to develop business opportunities in China.

These two companies' business model proved very successful over the years, first in France and then, abroad. Yet, they both face today a paradoxical situation: their development model is strongly criticized in their home country (by the consumer associations in particular), while it is becoming ever more successful and legitimate abroad. In addition, the advent of the European Union creates new contextual conditions to which they must adapt; for instance, French cities are beginning to open up all tenders to European, and not only French, competition, making the overall decision making, accountability and contractor allocating more transparent and competitive.

It is this that has led both companies to develop a new positioning with regard to their customers (the cities' mayor and council) and their customer's customers (the cities' citizens). They both decided to shift from the previous 'aménageur' positioning to a more distant, external one: that of 'collective services provider' for the Générale, and 'proximity collective

Example 4   *149*

services provider' for the Suez Lyonnaise. The objective is no longer to present themselves as 'city organizer', but rather as technical providers offering their various services to the city's elected council, who has the right to choose among different, competing technical offerings. Générale states it is organized around three major poles: Environment, Construction and Communication. Suez Lyonnaise presents itself as performing four major activities: Energy, Water, Waste Management and Communication. Such developments, whether structural or simply in terms of stated strategic positioning, represent a further step in how both firms relate competency and customer base development, a relationship one can expect they will further develop in the future.

Postscript

Upon finishing updating this example, we saw that the Compagnie Générale des Eaux announced it is changing its name to Vivendi. Vivendi is meant to reflect its strategic reorientation and its new role: that of supporting the quality of life of citizens.

References

af Petersens, F. and Bjurström, J., 1991, Identifying and analyzing 'intangible' assets, *M&A Europe*, September-October.

Argyris, C. and Schön, D., 1978, *Organizational Learning: a theory of action perspective*, London: Addison-Wesley.

Davis, S., 1987, *Future Perfect*, Reading, MA: Addison-Wesley.

Gershuny, J. and Miles, I., 1983, *The New Service Economy: the transformation of employment in industrial societies*, London: Frances Pinter.

Halberstam, D., 1986, *The Reckoning*, New York: William Morrow.

Hama, N., 1993, Strategy and the art of reinventing value, Perspectives Section, *Harvard Business Review*, September-October.

Hawking, S., 1991, *A Brief History of Time*, London: Bantam.

Hirschhorn, L., 1984, *Beyond Mechanisation*, Cambridge, MA: MIT Press.

Hirschhorn, L. and Gilmore, T., 1992, The new boundaries of the 'boundaryless' company, *Harvard Business Review*, May-June.

Morgan, G., 1986, *Images of Organization*, Beverly Hills, CA: Sage.

Normann, R., 1978, Development Strategies for Swedish Service Knowledge, *Report from Multi-client Study*, SIAR, Stockholm.

Normann, R., 1989, *Invadörernas Dans*, Stockholm: Liber.

Normann, R., [1984, 1st Edition] 1991, *Service Management*, 2nd edn, Chichester: Wiley.

Normann, R. and Ramírez, R., 1989, A theory of the offering: toward a neo-industrial business strategy, in Snow, C. C. (ed.), *Strategy, Organizational Design, and Human Resource Management*, Greenwich, CT: JAI Press.

Normann, R. and Ramírez, R., 1993a, From value chain to value constellation, *Harvard Business Review*, July-August.

Normann, R. and Ramírez, R., 1993b, Response in: Strategy and the Art of Creating Value, Perspectives Section, *Harvard Business Review*, September–October.

Pava, C., 1982, Microelectronics and the design of organization, Unpublished Harvard Business School Working Paper, HBS-82-67, April.

Pava, C., 1983, *Managing New Office Technology*, New York: Free Press.

Porter, M. E., 1985, *Competitive Advantage*, New York: Free Press.

Quinn, J. B. and Gagnon, C. E., 1986, Will services follow manufacturing into decline? *Harvard Business Review*, November-December.

Schön, D., 1971, *Beyond the Stable State*, New York: Random House.

Selznick, P., 1957, *Leadership in Administration*, New York: Harper and Row.

Smith, A., 1776, *The Wealth of Nations*, London: Stratton & Cadell.

Thompson, J. D., 1967, *Organizations in Action*, New York: McGraw-Hill.

Van der Heijden, K., 1993, Strategy and the art of reinventing value, Perspectives Section, *Harvard Business Review*, September-October.

Wickström, S. and Normann, R., 1993, *Knowledge and Value*, London: Routledge.

Glossary

Below, on the left column, is a list of the key terms which this book proposes. These help to understand value creation in the emerging neo-industrial business era. They are listed alphabetically; the numbers following them indicate the pages in which they are discussed. On the right column is a list of conventional terms from the industrial business era which the neo-industrial terms on the left column replace; or whose meaningfulness they re-define within the conceptual framework context which this book presents. Where new terms do not replace or re-define conventional terms, no 'counterpart' terms appear on the right-side column.

Terms considered to be more helpful in analysing neo-industrial business introduced in this book (in alphabetical order)	(Where relevant), conventional terms from the industrial economy era which the framework introduced in this book replaces or re-defines
Access (and access channel) 50, 52	Distribution system
Agricultural economy 11, 19	Agricultural (and primary) sector
Asset liquidity 18–21, 52	
Bundling and unbundling (of offerings) 53, 68, 81, 95	Pricing policy
Businesses we and our co-producers are in 29, 33, 42–3, 47–8, 77	Businesses we (alone) are in
Code system, code carrier 56–8	User or owner information guides; usability

Enabled co-production
94–5

Self-service

Enabling customers (through enabling offerings)
60–1

(in some situations) consulting or advising customers

Income carriers (*see also* bundling)
35–6

Priced vs. 'free' goods and services

Leverage value
56–7, 59–61, 68, 85–6, 120

Consumption and/or usufruct (value destruction)

Marching customer's value creation
78–81, 86

Client "needs"

Meta-competences
77–8, 81, 100, 101, 124, 145–7

Offerings
49, 52–3

Products, services

Price carrier (*see also* bundling)
35–6

Priced vs. 'free' goods and services

Reconfiguration
39–41, 73–6

Business and industry redefinition

Reconfiguration advantage
77

Competitive advantage

Relieving customers (through relieving offerings)
39–41, 60–1, 86, 87, 126

(in some situations) outsourcing

Value constellation
54–5, 76

Value chain

Index

Index compiled by Geoffrey C. Jones